BUILDING A

the strategic a
the ne

1   9

1·99

BUILDING A LITERATE NATION
the strategic agenda for literacy over the next five years

Edited by Neil McClelland
National Literacy Trust

Trentham Books

First published in 1997 by Trentham Books Limited

Trentham Books Limited
Westview House
734 London Road
Oakhill
Stoke on Trent
Staffordshire
England ST4 5NP

British Cataloguing in Publication Data
A catalogue record for this book is available from the British Library
ISBN 1 85856 085 3

Designed and typeset by Trentham Print Design Ltd., Chester and printed in Great Britain by Bemrose Shafron Ltd., Chester

CONTENTS

Part 2
Contributions from organisations in the literacy field

CONTRIBUTORS

INDIVIDUALS

Professor Michael Barber, Dean, New Initiatives Programme, Institute of Education, University of London and Chair of the Literacy Task Force

Dr. Roger Beard, Reader in Literacy Education, School of Education, University of Leeds

Dr. Greg Brooks, A full-time educational researcher and Vice-President Elect of the United Kingdom Reading Association

Dr. Martin Coles and **Christine Hall**, School of Education, University of Nottingham

Professor Henrietta Dombey, Professor of Literacy in Primary Education, School of Education, University of Brighton

Dr. Nigel Hall, School of Education, Manchester Metropolitan University

Dr. Peter Hannon, Director of the Raising Early Achievement in Literacy Project, Division of Education, University of Sheffield

Angela Hobsbaum, Reading Recovery National Network, Institute of Education, University of London

Professor Gunther Kress, Head of Culture Communication and Societies Group, Institute of Education, University of London

Jane Mace, Department of Educational Studies, Goldsmiths College, University of London

Professor Peter D. Pumfrey, Dean, School of Education, University of Manchester

Dr. Keith Topping, Director of the Centre for Paired Reading, Department of Psychology, University of Dundee

Professor Sheila Wolfendale, Director of the M.Sc./Doctorate in Educational Psychology Programme, Department of Psychology, University of East London

Dr. David Wray, Department of Education, University of Exeter

ORGANISATIONS

Adult Dyslexia Organisation (ADO)
Donald Schloss, Chairman and Melanie Jameson, Education Adviser

The Arts Council of England
Dr. Alastair Niven, Director of Literature

The Basic Skills Agency
Jim Pateman, Senior Development Officer

British Dyslexia Association
Paul Cann, Director

The British Film Institute
Cary Bazalgette, Principal Education Officer

Centre for Language in Primary Education
Dr. Myra Barrs, Director

The Dyslexia Institute
Liz Brooks, Executive Director

Federation of Children's Book Groups
Penny Dolan, Chair 1996/97

The Library Association
Ross Shimmon, Chief Executive

National Association for the Teaching of English
Anne Barnes, General Secretary

National Library for the Blind
Ilene Hoyle (National Library for the Blind) and Steve McCall, Birmingham University

National Literary Association
Charlie Griffiths, Project Director '99 by 99' Campaign

National Literacy Trust
Neil McClelland, Director

Northern Ireland Adult Literacy and Basic Education Committee (ALBEC)
Hilary A. Sloan, Chairperson

The Poetry Society
Alison Combes, Education Development Officer

Reading and Language Information Centre, University of Reading
Prue Goodwin and Viv Edwards

The Reading Reform Foundation
Dr. Bonnie Macmillan, Secretary of the UK Chapter

Research and Practice in Adult Literacy (RaPAL)
Mary Hamilton, Chair, Julia Clarke, Margaret Herrington, Gaye Houghton and David Barton

School Library Association
Graham Small, National Committee

Scottish Community Education Council (SCEC)
Charlie McConnell, Executive Director

United Kingdom Reading Association (UKRA)
Dr. Sue Beverton, President

Volunteer Reading Help (VRH)
Charles Martineau, Director

Foreword

Hardly a day goes by without some reference to literacy in the media, whether it concerns standards and teaching methods, funding requirements, reading habits, the critical role of parents and communities in supporting literacy or the importance of literacy for the United Kingdom's economic competitiveness.

The National Literacy Trust decided that it was time to bring together in one volume the perspectives and advice of the United Kingdom's literacy and literacy-related organisations, and of some leading thinkers and practitioners on *the strategic agenda for literacy over the next five years.*

The Trust has been delighted by the excellent response to its invitation to contribute to this book and thanks all those who have submitted contributions. It hopes that all the many recommendations and courses of action which are suggested will be carefully considered by local and central Government and other agencies, including the media. Whilst the Trust has provided the conduit for organisations and individuals to publish their views, it must be emphasised that the views expressed do not necessarily reflect the policy of the Trust.

The Trust also wishes to thank Delia Buckle and Jacky Taylor for all their skill and hard work in ensuring that the book became a reality.

Building a Literate Nation
- an Overview

The thirty six contributions contained in this volume demonstrate that literacy is a multi-faceted subject which commands the attention of practitioners and thinkers with very different perspectives, and involves a wide range of organisations serving and representing different client-groups. It is therefore not surprising that there is no common agenda for building a literate nation over the next five years.

What emerges strongly from several contributions is a recognition that literacy is a shared responsibility and there is a need to bring together all the different players in education, business, industry, the community and the family, so that resources and expertise are harnessed to the full. The solution which these contributors propose for building a literate nation is to form alliances or partnerships in order to establish a common agenda, and to coordinate the necessary resources to consider the different problems and overcome the separatism amongst professionals.

Another recurring need is to widen the definition of literacy to cover new forms of literacy in a digital age, such as on-screen literacy and moving image media, as well as print literacy. The importance is emphasised of ensuring access to the new electronic technologies and giving training and support for teachers and parents/carers in the use of information technology.

The literacy demands of the working, recreational and social worlds of today and tomorrow should be considered, as well as the impact of information-based economies on Western societies.

Some contributors are concerned about the media's presentation of literacy standards and teaching, and to challenge negative and simplistic images so as to focus on the positive. The need is indicated for a national monitoring system. Some contributors advocate a light sample system. Others argue for national targets for children's literacy. Some want the ways in which the National Curriculum assists or hinders the development of good literacy skills to be reviewed and more space in the curriculum for teaching and learning literacy. The case is argued for poets in schools and the role of poetry in the curriculum.

The importance of home-school partnerships and family literacy programmes is recognised by a number of contributors. Parents/carers and other adults in the local community are seen as an untapped source who can support and help children. Measures are recommended for promoting literacy in the pre-school period, beginning with babies.

Primary school teachers are seen by some contributors as the main resource on which the improvement of literacy depends over the next five years. Greater support for teachers is urged, with continuing professional development and in-service training. Others want to see the reform or overhaul of teacher training so that teachers at both primary and secondary level are better equipped to teach reading, writing and spelling.

The importance of preventive measures and programmes which allow children, young people and adults to catch up and improve their skills is also stressed. Measures are put forward to help those with special needs. Consideration is also given to the social and gender issues involved in reading failure and how they can be tackled.

The range of recommendations on funding priorities include pre-school education, smaller classes in primary schools, supplementary funding for bilingual children and children in areas of social need, family literacy, remedial programmes for adults and children, and more adequate funding for adult literacy.

Concerns are expressed about insufficient resources for textbooks and other publications. The school library service should be strengthened and some advocate making it a mandatory service.

An abundance of ideas and projects is put forward for further investigation and research in the field of literacy. Some contributors advise on the need for the strategic agenda for literacy to develop a range of remedial approaches and not to rely on a blanket approach. As one contributor says: 'There are no quick fixes, no pedagogic panaceas, no soundbite solutions to help build a literate nation'.

Perhaps the message for the nation's policy makers is to give careful consideration to all the advice and recommendations which have been put forward and to endorse the words of one contributor: 'Many organisations, agencies and individuals will need to be mobilised to ensure a high-level, not a half-hearted, response. And there will be a need for Government, national and local, to take a lead in supporting and co-ordinating what must be a national campaign'.

Part I

Contributions from leading thinkers and practitioners in the literacy field

1
Transforming Standards of Literacy

Michael Barber

Institute of Education, University of London and Chair of the Literacy Task Force

Everyone wants higher standards of literacy. The politicians recognise that it is the key to achievement in school and that higher standards of performance at the end of compulsory education are essential preconditions for economic success and social harmony. Business people, too, want them to be higher. Parents of course want their children to learn to read.

But the people who want higher literacy standards most are primary teachers. They know more than anyone the joy of watching a child grasp the skills of reading; of seeing a child find out about the real world, and many imaginary ones too, through books. And they know the pain, worry and frustration when, in spite of their best efforts, a child does not learn to read. There are few groups in society more self-critical than primary teachers and few things more likely to burden them with guilt than a child who does not learn to read.

Yet, in spite of these shared good intentions the evidence suggests that reading standards are not rising and may even be falling slightly. Reports by both OFSTED and the Secondary Heads' Association within the last year have heightened concern. The last systematic attempt to look at reading standards over time was made by the NFER for the National Commission on Education in 1994. It concluded that standards now are roughly the same as they were thirty years ago.

While this may scotch the view that there has been a drastic decline over the last generation, it is disturbing nevertheless. We would be appalled if we were asked now to accept 1960s standards in, for example, broadcasting or medicine. Moreover standards must rise continuously if we are to keep up with the international competition and give children the skills they will need to thrive in the 21st century. Remaining the same is not an option. We have to do better.

We will not transform literacy standards by berating teachers. Nor will we do so by thinking up superficially attractive palliatives which grab a fleeting headline.

Instead we need to set an ambitious target which, if achieved, would bring us into line with the best in the world. We then need to work towards it on the basis of a strategy in which government, teachers, employers and parents can have confidence. We need to base our approach on the best research we have about how to teach reading. We need to implement the strategy with care. And we need to stick to it for at least five years.

Literacy Task Force

In a nutshell, showing a government how all this could be done is the task that David Blunkett has given the Literacy Task Force which he set up in May 1996. The target he has suggested is that every child should be able to read well by the age of eleven, unless they have a specified special educational need. Put another way, he would like to see virtually all 11 year olds achieve Level 4, the National Curriculum level expected of 11 year olds.

The target is rightly and necessarily ambitious. The 1995 National Curriculum tests revealed just how far there is to go. Seven per cent of eleven year olds recorded Level 5, 41 per cent Level 4, 39 per cent Level 3 and 9 per cent Levels 1 or 2 (4 per cent were unavailable).

The 1996 results showed significant progress but 42 per cent still fell below Level 4 and the huge variation in performance around the average remains a cause for major concern.

Since the establishment of the Task Force I have received a flood of correspondence, overwhelmingly from primary teachers. It reveals a sense of excitement at the prospect of working together, on the basis of a shared strategy, towards an ambitious national target. There is a refreshing lack of complacency. It also reveals vividly the two areas in which primary teachers believe they need most help.

Areas in which primary school teachers need help

Firstly, there is a real thirst for more knowledge about how best to teach reading. It would seem from the correspondence that most primary teachers have not had the training they need in the latest developments in the techniques of teaching reading, unless they happen to have worked in a school where the head is well-read in, for example, the new phonics. Unless this issue is systematically attacked across the country there can be little hope of solving our literacy problems. The work of John Stannard and the new literacy centres has so far been excellent. Once their new approach has been tested in schools from early 1997, we shall have a growing body of experience on which to base future decisions.

Secondly, teachers want to know more about how best to help children who can read learn to read well. Put in the blunt terms of the KS2 tests the question they are raising is: how can the 39 per cent of children who achieve Level 3 be enabled to achieve Level 4? This was one of the central challenges that faced the Literacy Task Force, and indeed the country as a whole; yet in the popular debate about the teaching of reading it barely figures at all.

The Task Force sought to develop the skills of the whole primary teaching force.

The Task Force also sought to clarify parents' responsibilities.

The Task Force published its report entitled, '*A Reading Revolution: How We Can Teach Every Child To Read*' in February 1997. It sets out the most ambitious strategy ever to raise standards of literacy in primary schools. The strategy for solving the problems which contribute to present poor performance includes the following:

A National Approach to Reading

- For the first time, there will be national recommendations on how to teach reading based on OFSTED and international research evidence of what works. All of this shows that a strong element of phonics and direct teaching of literacy are important. The report recommends a minimum one hour literacy lesson every day. The literacy hour would include a combination of fast-paced, whole-class teaching and follow-up group work. An independent evaluation of the government's National Literacy Project, alongside the most successful international evidence, will provide the information on which to base the national recommendations

Teacher Development

- All courses for training primary teachers will be covered by a National Curriculum for teacher education, which will emphasise phonics and the literacy hour. Courses will be required to spend twice as long on the teaching of reading as they do now (i.e. 100 hours instead of 50). This would bring us into line with New Zealand, a country renowned for its success in promoting literacy

- By the end of the school year 1998-9, a national programme for ensuring all 190,000 primary teachers know how to teach reading will have been implemented

Literacy Inspection

- In the year following the completion of the national programme for primary teachers (1999-2000), standards of teaching reading should be much higher. To check the impact of the programme, there will be short inspections of literacy performance in a 10 per cent sample of primary schools

- A new award will be introduced for primary schools which are able to demonstrate that they are managing and teaching literacy in accordance with best practice. This will be based on the Basic Skills Agency Quality Mark which is already being developed

Reading Recovery

- Once every school is teaching literacy in accordance with best practice, reading recovery should play a part in assisting six-year-olds who nevertheless fall behind their peers, to catch up. Ways should be found to make it more cost-effective than it is at present

A More Focused National Curriculum

• The National Curriculum for primary schools, when it is revised for September 2000, should become more closely focused on the three 'Rs' and give teachers much greater discretion outside the core

Parents

• Home-school agreements and national guidelines on homework will recommend that all parents of primary age children read with their children for 20 minutes each day. Ideally, parents should meet their child's teacher at least every six months to review progress and set targets for future progress in literacy

A National Year of Reading

• The school year 1998-9 will be the National Year of Reading. It will be a major campaign, intended to involve every parent and every citizen. A range of media slots, activities etc. will ensure that every citizen knows about it and is encouraged to take part. The idea would be to encourage parents and other adults to play their part in helping to raise expectations and standards of literacy. A number of major organisations have already expressed strong support for this initiative

Managing the Strategy

• The national strategy will be overseen and co-ordinated by a Literacy Strategy Group based in the Department for Education and Employment and involve all the national agencies, including the Teacher Training Agency, Office for Standards in Education, Basic Skills Agency and QNCA, as well as leading professionals

• LEAs will be expected to support the national literacy strategy and to appoint between 2 and 5 literacy consultants, which the 13 LEAs in the present government's National Literacy Project have done. Inspection of LEAs will give high priority to assessing their impact on raising standards of literacy.

Raising literacy standards is a job for parents, business and the media as well as teachers. If we want a successful society in the 21st Century, then everyone must take literacy seriously. Together we can transform standards of literacy. If we have a sense of ambition and find a means of unlocking the power of collective endeavour, there will be no stopping us.

2
Creating Space for Literacy

Roger Beard

School of Education, University of Leeds

The broader context of standards and social change

It is nearly 25 years since work began on drawing up an earlier strategic agenda for literacy, through the setting up of the Bullock Committee.[1] There are advantages in returning to the work of that Committee whose report, *A Language for Life*, was eventually published in 1975. It may still have lessons for us and also remind us how a new agenda has to take account of the social change of the past quarter century.

Then, as now, there were concerns about national standards. The monitoring of educational standards is beset with uncertainties. Tests that seemed appropriate in one era seem less valid in another, as test items begin to show their age. The steady increase in the reading standards of eleven year olds in the 1950s and 60s was identified by tests that contained references to 'wheelwright' and 'mannequin parade'.[2] Yet, as tests are replaced in order to reflect more valid content and contemporary language use, so new baselines have to be established and comparisons with the past become far less easy to make.

One way around this dilemma is to use a system of item-banking. A series of equivalent tests can be constructed for use over a long period and aging test items can be discarded as new combinations are put together. Once a baseline is established, only light sampling of schools is required. It was unfortunate that, after a decade of work by the Assessment of Performance Unit,[3] set up in the light of the Bullock Committee's recommendations for improved national monitoring, such a programme was ended. The decision was presumably taken in the belief that national standards could be monitored by the use of the more recently developed Standard Assessment Tasks (SATs). However, anyone who has observed the rapidly changing content and formats of these tests since their inception will recognise how unsuitable they are for monitoring changes in national standards. Not only have they been based on two different versions of a National Curriculum, but they have used different kinds of information. First, varying combinations of specific criteria were used; later, broad descriptions of attainment levels.

Reinstating a programme of national monitoring

All this means that any strategic agenda for literacy has to be considered in a national context which is not being monitored in the way that might be expected in an advanced country like Britain. Thus there is much to be said for beginning the agenda with a plea for the reinstatement of the work of the APU, or its equivalent. This would enable other aspects of the agenda to be set against information on standards which is more reliable than SATs data and more valid than the subjective impressions of individual commentators. The need for such monitoring has become even more pressing because the social change of recent years has profoundly altered the contexts in which children's literacy can be fostered: in their home life, in what they tackle in the school curriculum and in the leisure opportunities which are available to them. A common feature is that there has been a *loss of space*: space in children's lives in which books can be shared, in which literacy can be learned and in which related leisure interests can be pursued. An agenda for literacy needs to be aimed at reclaiming some of this space in the home and the school.

Making the most of the bedtime story

It is difficult to improve upon the recommendations of the Bullock Report in this respect, that the best advice to give to parents of young children is for them to hold their children on their laps and read aloud to them stories which they like, over and over again.[4] It is also difficult to obtain information on how common this practice still is. The past quarter century has certainly seen some developments that threaten the bedtime story. Children are now more likely to have a television in their bedroom and, when this does not offer a serious distraction, the hand-held computer game can provide its own compulsive appeal. Combined with the significant increase in the numbers of children who live in homes where both parents work, as well as other major increases in 'workaholicism' in those who are in work and the distractions of long-term unemployment in those who are not, then it would seem all too likely that children are not read to as often as they once were.

A recent American research review calculated that, if children also share in a range of word games like I-Spy, are taught rhymes and jingles and are involved in the purposeful use of print around the home, then they can take advantage of as much as 1000 hours of literacy learning before they even begin school.[5] Of all these activities, the bedtime story has a particularly cohesive part to play. Parent, child, restfulness and comfort are brought together with the kinds of vicarious experience which only books can offer and with the infinite range of ideas which texts can so effectively promote.[6] It behoves everyone in literacy education to help parents to recognise the importance of bedtime stories for children of all ages and to make the most of the time and the books which are available.

Cutting back the National Curriculum

The school curriculum has lost space for the teaching and learning of literacy. Anyone who has watched a teacher of five-year-old children filling in a ten subject report form for each child in the class is likely to ask, quite simply, whether we are asking our primary teachers to try to teach too much, too soon. The Bullock Report offered many suggestions for improving literacy education, some of which remain unfulfilled.[7] It is curious that, rather than build strategically upon the work of that Committee (and the work of the Cockcroft Committee for Mathematics), national policy has been to introduce a whole new range of subjects from the very beginnings of compulsory schooling.

Despite the recent slimming down of the National Curriculum, there are still many indications that our teachers are battling just to hear children read. Excessive curriculum demands continue to eat into the time in which teachers might otherwise have been able to read to children, to encourage them to think critically about stories and information, to model how texts are organised and to show how the phonology of our language maps on to its spelling system. Although the National Curriculum has been in place for nearly a decade, it is important that its overall structure does not become taken for granted. Other countries may have taken a more sensible approach from which we may have much to learn. There is a noticeable contrast between the stressful circumstances in which literacy is being taught in British schools and reports of teaching in New Zealand, for instance, where substantially more teachers' time is devoted to literacy teaching.[8]

Toward a strategic agenda

Reading to children, further reducing the National Curriculum and reinstating a system of national monitoring: these are key items for an agenda that reflects the fact that parents, professional educators and policy makers all have their part to play in building a literate nation.

Notes

1   DES (1975) *A Language for Life* (The Bullock Report) London: HMSO

2   See Beard, R. (1990) *Developing Reading 3-13* London: Hodder and Stoughton, pp. 258-260

3   APU (Assessment of Performance Unit) (1988) *Language Performance in Schools* London: HMSO

4   DES (1975) *A Language for Life* (The Bullock Report) London: HMSO, p.97

5   Adams, M.J. (1990) *Beginning to Read* Cambridge, Mass.: MIT Press

6   See Heath, S.B. (1982) 'What No Bedtime Story Means: Narrative Skills at Home and School', *Language and Society*, 11, 49-76

7   Examples include ways of extending and developing reading in the later years of primary schooling, according to recent Ofsted Reviews of Inspection Findings in English. See also Beard, R. (1990) *Developing Reading 3-13*, chapters 8 and 9.

8   Office for Standards in Education (Ofsted) (1993) *Reading Recovery in New Zealand* London: HMSO

3

The Case for National Monitoring

Greg Brooks

A full-time educational researcher and Vice-President-Elect of the United Kingdom Reading Association writes here in a personal capacity

On 21 November 1996 two educational reports were published simultaneously: the 'league tables' of GCSE and A-Level results for schools in England in 1996 (the fifth such set of data), and the first volume of the national results for England of the Third International Mathematics and Science Study, which was carried out in 1995. On the basis of the first of these two sets of results, it was claimed by some commentators that standards of educational achievement had risen over the previous five years; on the basis of the second set of results, it was claimed by other commentators that standards of achievement in mathematics had *fallen* since the previous international study in 1991.

And each August for the last several years, the rise in the proportion of 16-year-olds achieving grade C or better in five or more GCSEs has been simultaneously claimed as showing that standards are rising, because pupils get better grades, and as showing that they are falling, in the sense that the grade C/D boundary, or 'pass-level', must have been lowered. This dispute applies at least as much to literacy as to other subjects, and perhaps more so.

How can we know what the trend of literacy standards is? Who is right, the optimists or the pessimists? The answer is that nobody knows.

In England and Wales there is at present no system specifically intended to monitor the trend of educational standards over time. There are of course the public examinations at ages 16 and 18, and national tests in maths and English at age 7, and in these subjects and science at ages 11 and 14. But the primary purpose of these systems is to deliver individual-level information on the performance of each child taking the tests on a particular occasion, and not to provide national information on the performance of the education service as a whole even on each occasion, let alone over time.

When plans for national tests were first announced, one of the Government's stated intentions for them was that they should provide a basis for monitoring trends over time; but this was trammelled with several other purposes – the tests were also to be formative, summative and diagnostic, and to provide professional development.

This was too wide-ranging a set of objectives for one assessment system to achieve; yet even after the Dearing review implicitly abandoned the formative and diagnostic aims, the range of purposes of national tests still officially encompassed summative purposes and, by implication, a monitoring system:

> National tests have ... a summative purpose. They are undertaken in order to contribute to an objective view of pupils' achievements ... at the end of key stages 1, 2 and 3. The information they supply can then be reported to parents and can be used to help form judgements about the progress being made by the class, the school *and the education system as a whole*. (Dearing, 1993, para. 5.9, my italics)

It seems to me that this still leaves the national tests with two purposes which it is in practice very difficult, if not logically impossible, for one system to deliver simultaneously. The reason why this is difficult also applies to GCSE results, and arises from the high-stakes nature of both assessment systems. Where an assessment makes a public difference to children's lives, or at least to the standing of their schools, it is both understandable and inevitable that teachers will teach to the form and thrust of the test, because teachers know that their pupils cannot give of their best if they are inadequately prepared. But this also inevitably means that the tests used in any one year cannot be kept secure: new tests are needed every year. This leads to the difficulties, which the examination boards openly recognise, of keeping the 'standard' (pass-mark or average or whatever statistic is being used) steady from year to year.

And even if the examiners succeed in doing that, and the proportions of children achieving certain levels still rise from year to year, is that because their attainment is actually better, or because their teachers are getting better at preparing their pupils for the test, or because the nature of the test or examination is subtly shifting, or because of some mixture of these? Does a rise, or a fall, in these results tell us anything about children's underlying ability in literacy or numeracy or whatever subject is being tested?

To my mind, the only method which offers the hope of obtaining reliable data on the last question is to have a separate, single-purpose, light-sample monitoring system which is independent of the pressures of public examinations and national tests. Such a system is low-stakes – so no-one has anything to gain or lose from it and the tests used can be kept secure. They can then be re-used, thus eliminating one source of irrelevant variation when estimating trends over time. Such a 'repeated tests' design is not without its own problems, but they are at least as manageable as those of a national testing system when that is expected also to deliver individual-pupil-level information.

Scotland does have such a monitoring system, in the form of the Assessment of Academic Progress (AAP), which mounts surveys of English, mathematics and science in a three-year cycle. In Northern Ireland, the first step towards establishing a monitoring system has been taken with the commissioning of surveys of reading standards in 1993 and 1996.

In England and Wales, surveys of reading performance of pupils aged 11 and 15 were undertaken at roughly four-year intervals from 1948 to 1979; then between 1979 and 1988 the Assessment of Performance Unit (APU) mounted surveys of reading and writing at these ages on six occasions. Neither system worked perfectly as a monitoring device, the pre-APU surveys because the tests were inadequate reflections of the full range of literacy attainment, the APU because of disputes over the appropriate statistical models to use (see Foxman, Hutchison and Bloomfield, 1991, especially chapter 15). Since the abolition of the APU in 1990, all that has happened in England and Wales is that the National Foundation for Educational Research has mounted surveys of reading performance at age 8 in 1991 (Gorman and Fernandes, 1992) and 1995 (Brooks, Shagen *et al.*, 1997) and at age 9 in 1996 (Brooks, Pugh and Schagen, 1996). These provided independent evidence that the average standard of 8-year-olds had fallen between 1987 and 1991, then returned to the 1987 level by 1995; and that the 9-year-olds tested in 1996 had made slow progress over the previous 12 months, and ranked within the middle group of countries which had used the same test internationally in 1991. Such findings are essential to an informed debate about the trend of literacy standards, yet none of this work was funded by central government. It seems illogical that England and Wales should not have a government-funded, single-purpose monitoring system.

The basic reason for national monitoring was stated with clarity some 20 years ago:

There will always be keen interest in the movement of standards, and it is perfectly natural that there should be. Where there is no information there will be speculation, and the absence of facts makes room for prejudice... Information of the right quality will be of value to teachers and researchers and will be a reference point for policy decisions at the level of central and local government. (Department of Education and Science, 1975, p.36).

It is high time for national educational monitoring to be re-started in England and Wales. Only by doing this can some clarity be restored to the national debate over the trend of educational standards, both in literacy and more widely.

References

Brooks, G., Pugh, A.K. and Schagen, I. (1996) *Reading Performance at Nine*. Slough: NFER.

Brooks, G., Schagen, I., Nastat, P., Lilly, J., Othman, Y. and Papadopoulou, CH.-O. (1997) *Trends in Reading at Eight*. Slough: NFER.

Dearing, R. (1993) *Interim Report on the National Curriculum*. London: Department of Education and Science.

Department of Education and Science (1975) *A Language for Life*. (The Bullock Report). London: HMSO.

Foxman, D. Hitchison, D. and Bloomfield, B. (1991) *The APU Experience*. London: School Examinations and Assessment Council.

Gorman, T.P. and Fernandes, C. (1992) *Reading in Recession*. Slough: NFER.

4

Building on Children's Reading Choices

Martin Coles and Christine Hall

School of Education, University of Nottingham

The Children's Reading Choices Project

In 1971 in England the Schools Council commissioned an enquiry which sought to discover the extent and kind of children's voluntary reading. A national questionnaire survey was conducted by the University of Sheffield under the direction of Frank Whitehead (Whitehead, 1977) with some 8000 children of 10, 12 and 14 years old.

It is now over twenty years since we acquired detailed information on children's voluntary reading habits. In those two decades there have been dramatic shifts in children's leisure habits and interests and in the cultural climate generally. One of the recommendations of the 1971 survey was that similar surveys should be carried out at ten year intervals, and it seemed important to us, especially in the light of current political concerns about reading generally, that monitoring of children's reading habits should continue. We set out therefore to replicate the Whitehead study in the context of the 1990s. A national questionnaire survey was conducted with 7976 children of 10, 12 and 14 years old in 110 primary (5-11 years) and 59 secondary (11-16/18 years) schools in 1994. We used a stratified random sample so selected that the findings could be generalised to the total relevant populations of children in England. To supplement the questionnaire, follow-up interviews were conducted in July 1995 with just over 1% of the sample in different schools throughout the country.

This contribution reports the findings of that project, the *W. H. Smith Children's Reading Choices Project*, the largest in-depth study of children's voluntary reading in the U.K. since Whitehead's and draws some conclusions which should inform the current and future agenda for literacy. It is divided into two parts. We will summarise the main findings and then, briefly, offer some suggestions about the implications of our study for teachers, parents, policy makers and for further research.

Main findings

The 'headline' findings then are these:

- Over the last two decades reported book reading has increased for 10 year olds of both sexes, and for 12 year old girls. It has remained at the same level for 12 year old boys and for 14 year old girls. It has declined for 14 year old boys

- The average number of books reported as read by children in the four weeks prior to the survey was 2.52 which compares with a figure of 2.40 in 1971

- Most children report regular reading, but there is a tendency towards fewer books being read as children get older

- More girls than boys read books regularly

- There is a clear pattern of decline in the amount of book reading from higher to lower socio-economic groups

- Children have eclectic reading tastes

- Children of any one age are reading books of markedly different levels of sophistication

- Children's 'classics' are still being widely read

- Children enjoy reading series of books

- The media have a strong influence on children's reading choices

- Very few children read only non-fiction, but seventy-eight percent of those that do are boys

- Adventure stories are the most popular genre at all ages and for both sexes

- One third of children in the survey had re-read one or more books

- Magazines, comics and newspapers are widely read by children of all ages. Twenty-four per cent of the sample regularly read five or more periodicals

- Most children view reading positively and have positive views of themselves as readers

- Children read more books and have a more positive view of their abilities as readers if they live with a sibling who they consider reads a lot. For both boys and girls the influence of having other children at home who read seems to be more important than the influence of having keen adult readers at home

- Children who speak a language other than English at home read slightly more than other children

- Reading material is more often purchased from newsagents, general stores and supermarkets than from bookshops

- Over 90% of children from all social groups report owning their own books

- Over 70% of children say they borrow books from the Public Library

- Children who read the most watch least television

- Approximately two thirds of all children had done some reading in the evening previous to the survey. The amount of reading children do in the evening decreases with age

- There is no significant relationship between the amount of time children claim to spend in computer use and the amount of time they claim to spend reading

Discussion

This is the headline information. What do we make of it? We want to draw attention briefly to nine particular inferences we make from our findings which should inform debates about literacy.

- Firstly these are generally encouraging findings. Popular fears that an increase in other distractions for children in the 1990s has led to an overall decline in the amount of book reading are, using these figures, unfounded. As well as an increase in book reading, newspaper and magazine reading has increased amongst children over the twenty year period since the Whitehead survey. The fact that there is a good deal of re-reading taking place suggests that children are enjoying their books and returning to them as sources of interest, enjoyment or comfort (or all three).

• For boys a statistically significant increase in the amount of reading compared to the 1971 findings at 10+ becomes neutral at 12+ and a significant decrease at 14+. For girls a statistically significant increase at 10+ and 12+ becomes neutral at 14+. What both sets of figures above show of course is that boys have been reading less than girls for the last 25 years. This is not a new phenomenon. It would be simplistic however to make a direct link between these figures and the well-documented under-achievement in school of boys compared to girls. The school achievement of boys relates to a complex of factors. Reading patterns might well be one of those factors, so an attempt to develop boys' reading habits through a careful look at what they *do* choose to read as they get older seems to us a sensible way forward. Our figures suggest primary schools are having some success in encouraging boys to read, so an analysis of the successes in improving reading amongst younger boys also seems to us a potentially profitable line of research.

• Although enthusiastic readers are to be found across both sexes and in all social groups, there is a clear pattern of decline in the amount of book reading from higher to lower socio-economic groups. Since the numbers of books which children say they own declines steadily from social group A to social group D/E, and since analysis of periodical purchase suggests a pattern of buying limited only by purchasing power, it is likely that this finding is explained as much by economic as by cultural factors. These findings might be laid alongside others such as the NFER study *Reading In Recession* (1992) which concluded that there had indeed been a small but significant drop in the reading performance of pupils in the previous decade, but that lower standards are not general throughout the system. Thirty-seven per cent of the schools in their sample had raised their scores. All were in shire counties, rural areas or in middle-class suburbs of larger conurbations. So we simply point out what perhaps should be obvious: that in drawing conclusions from such reports as ours it is not enough to consider the education system alone. We must look too at the circumstances of economic need and social disadvantage in which many of our children still live.

• Teachers, parents and librarians ought to be aware that, left to choose their own reading material, children have eclectic reading tastes, that the range of books being read by children of any one age is notable, and that children from different social groups do not have tastes that accord to stereotype. For instance, 'horror' titles are named by a far higher percentage of children in social group A than in any other group. Children from lower socio-economic groups (D/E and C_2) are proportionally more likely to be reading poetry. Importantly too, very few significant differences emerge between one broad group and another when the questions are considered in relation to ethnicity.

• Given the connection between self-esteem and achievement, there is good news in the findings of the project. If we consider the evidence that children with low self-esteem as readers are less likely to read, and therefore to exacerbate any difficulties or sense of failure they might be experiencing, it is heartening to note that even those who read least are likely to consider themselves of at least average ability as readers.

• The finding that for both boys and girls the influence of having other children who read at home is more important than the influence of having adults who read a lot, taken with the finding that children are more influenced by peers in their reading choices than by adults, has direct implications for teachers and Family Literacy Projects. The important emphasis which is often given to the parental role in encouraging children's reading should perhaps be supplemented by attention to encouraging collaborative activities with siblings and peers.

• The findings are positive in relation to speakers of languages other than English. These children have very positive views of themselves as readers, read slightly more books and magazines than others, and use the library significantly more than others. However half of these children say that finding reading material in their 'home' language is difficult. Despite strenuous efforts on the part of some schools and LEAs, it is clear that there is a continuing need for publishers, libraries and schools to recognise languages other than English in the provision of reading material.

• Fears that television and computer use are working to the detriment of literacy are not supported by these findings. Although children who read the most watch the least television, there is no suggestion that using a computer or watching a lot of television prevents children from reading books. Nearly 20% of those who claimed to have read more than seven books over the four week period of the survey, also claim to have watched more than three and a half hours of television in one evening. Indeed films and television series create a demand for associated products, which include books, and there are a large number of computer magazines being read by children in our sample.

• And finally our findings, both from the questionnaire and interviews, suggest a major feature of children's reading is one that is often unrecognised by adults. Large numbers of children are motivated to buy, swap and read magazines. For educationalists concerned about promoting children's reading development, therefore, periodical reading needs to be taken seriously. Magazines and newspapers provide important sources of information and advice and play a significant part in young people's reading. We need to be clear about what and how children are reading – not in order to invade their private reading spaces, but in order to build upon the foundations they have laid, to extend their range of reading strategies and the type of material they consider.

References

T. Gorman and C. Fernandez (1992) *Reading in Recession*, Slough: NFER

F. Whitehead (1977) *Children and Their Books: the final report of the Schools Council research project on children's reading habits, 10-15*, London: Macmillan.

5

A Strategic Agenda for Literacy over the next Five Years

Henrietta Dombey

School of Education, University of Brighton

Where are we now?

Press coverage over the past few years has painted a picture of incompetent teachers and declining standards across the educational board with particularly dire effects in reading. But research evidence suggests a rather different reality. Certainly mean scores for the reading of seven to eight year olds fell between the mid-to-late eighties, although since 1991 these are back up to the mid-eighties level (Brooks, Nastat et al., 1996). However, currently, mean scores at nine put us only thirteenth in the league table of countries participating in the IEA's survey, well below Finland and New Zealand although not far behind Germany or the Netherlands (Elley, 1992). What marks us out from these and other countries is our 'long tail of under-achievement' (Brooks, Pugh and Schagen, 1996).

Indeed, over the years of decline the scores of higher and mid-achievers held up, while this tail of under-achievement grew fatter, dragging the mean scores down (Lake, 1991; Gorman and Fernandes, 1992). These two studies associate this tail with poverty. Britain now leads Europe in the gap created between the better off and those living in poverty: in the key five years between 1985 and 1990, the number of children officially designated as living in poverty quadrupled from 40,000 to 160,000 (DSS 1995). It's still rising. Poverty rather than incompetent teaching seems to be responsible for our tail of under-achievement.

Sales of children's books have been rising steadily and, despite cutbacks, there has been expansion too in the number loaned by public libraries (Fishwick, 1995, LISU, 1994). The news on reading is not all bad.

What do we need?

But meanwhile the demands made on our literacy – as employees, citizens, and members of special interest groups – increase inexorably, as we are bombarded daily with an increasing number of ever more complex texts. If we are to make our mark on this complex world, by and large this must be done through literate means. Those who leave school without having put literacy to work for them risk being pushed ever further to society's margins. The citizens of the next millennium need a complex, wide-ranging, flexible and critical literacy. So our agenda should widen our view of literacy as well as provide support for its development.

National monitoring and formative assessment

We need a system of monitoring, independent of government control, more searching than both conventional tests of reading and writing and also the cumbersome machinery associated with the national curriculum. We need to address the literacy demands of the working, recreational and social worlds of today and tomorrow, involving such matters as:

- how well children establish literal meaning from texts

- how well they work out inferential meanings

- how well they relate what they read to what they have learned elsewhere

- how critical children are of what they read and write

- what children do with their reading and writing at different stages

- how much children read and write

- how much they like reading and writing

- their effectiveness as readers and writers of a range of text types, including video, other visual text and interactive multi-media.

For a fraction of the cost of the current National Curriculum assessment procedures, light sampling could give a multi-dimensional picture of children's literacy.

Meanwhile teacher assessment needs to be given a clear role and a proper status, through an instrument that, as well as attending to these aspects of literacy learning, focuses also on how individual children can be helped forward, and includes the perspectives of parents and children. The Primary Language Record provides an excellent model for a system that should be introduced nationally (Barrs et al., 1988).

Resources for school and pre-school education

Effective education in literacy is not cheap. Children in 'normal' situations need:

• nursery education, to equip them socially, imaginatively and intellectually for the demands of formal schooling

• teachers well qualified in literacy teaching;

• classes small enough to ensure the necessary attention for everyone

• a plentiful supply of printed texts as attractive as those children see outside school

• access, from their earliest years, to computers with suitable software including interactive multimedia.

Some children need more. The last fifteen years have seen the progressive withdrawal of supplementary funding for bilingual children and children in areas of social difficulty. If 'the long tail of underachievement' is to be reduced, such children need:

• smaller class sizes and the qualified extra teaching and support staff to allow their teachers to get on with the job of teaching

• continuity of teaching from able teachers with high expectations of them.

Support for teachers

Teachers need to feel they are respected and supported, not constantly harried and disparaged. Rather than being subjected to increasingly detailed curricular requirements in literacy (Ofsted, 1996) teachers need to be helped to develop:

- their knowledge and understanding of the processes of reading and writing – how they work and what they are good for

- their judgement and inventiveness about children, texts, social contexts, learning opportunities and their own teaching interventions.

This means that as well as support from colleagues in school, teachers need challenge from courses of continued professional education, that are not narrowly instrumental, but foster a greater intellectual understanding of literacy and literacy learning, and a greater professional self-awareness.

Access to texts

If we are to develop a critical wide-ranging literacy, children and adults need access to texts. All schools and colleges should be given inducements to set up bookshops, with saving schemes that encourage maximum participation in book buying. The *Reading Is Fundamental* project should be extended to all areas of poverty, ensuring that all children can possess books.

For the written word to bind us together instead of dividing us, public libraries need to reconstruct a central role in the literacy of the twenty-first century. After many years of decline, they need to renew their book stocks and remedy staff cuts. And, as well as providing access to the Internet they also need to give access to interactive multi-media.

Working with families

We need to extend systematically the many successful initiatives, such as the Sheffield project, that help parents exploit the learning opportunities of their homes (Hannon, 1996). Once their children are in school, parents need to be treated by teachers as fully collaborative partners in the business of assessing and developing children's literacy.

Like school literacy, adult literacy needs better funding. Schemes must recognise the literacy practices that govern their students' lives, help them to engage in these actively and to use literacy to move beyond their immediate worlds. We should encourage more initiatives which attend both to adults' own literacy and the support they can provide for their children's literacy learning.

Research

Literacy and literacy learning have been much researched. We know far more than we did twenty years ago about such matters as literacy learning before school, the phonics lessons children need to learn, the cultural dimensions of literacy and literacy learning, and what children do when they read. But we still know all too little about how successful teachers engage children in productive learning, and have virtually no useful information on the comparative effectiveness of different approaches to literacy teaching. These matters are far from straightforward, as there is much room for controversy over the criteria by which success is determined. But if teachers are to be helped to develop more effective ways of teaching their children, such questions must be tackled.

Media

There is an urgent need to work on the media presentation of literacy, to ensure that journalists are aware that standards are not slipping right across the board, and to increase their understanding of literacy learning so that they see and present it as a vastly complex enterprise, stretching from children's first encounters with texts, through their slowly developing awareness of speech as sound, to an ability to make sense of a vast range of texts for a vast variety of purposes, some of which pose problems for very many adults today. Above all we must help journalists to focus on the positive, and demonstrate that there are many cheering lessons to be learned from our classrooms.

References

Barrs, M et al. (1988) *The Primary Language Record – Teachers' Handbook* London: Centre for Language in Primary Education

Brooks, G, Nastat, P., et al. (1996) *Trends in Reading at Eight*, Slough: National Foundation for Educational Research

Brooks, G, Pugh, AK and Schagen (1996) *Reading Performance at Nine*, Slough: National Foundation for Educational Research and the Open University

Department of Social Security (1995) *Households Below Average Income: A statistical analysis*, London: DSS

Elley, WB (1992) How in the World do Students Read? Hamburg: International Association for the Evaluation of Educational Achievement

Fishwick, F (1995) *The Book Trade Yearbook*, London: The Publishers' Association

Gorman, TP, Fernandes, C, (1992) *Reading in Recession*, Slough: National Foundation for Educational Research

Hannon, P (1995) *Literacy Home And School: Research and practice in teaching with parents*, London: Falmer

Lake, M (1991) 'Surveying all the factors: reading research', *Language and Learning* 6

Library and Information Statistics Unit (1995) *Annual Library Statistics*, Loughborough: Loughborough University

6

Going Forward into the Past

Nigel Hall

School of Education, Manchester Metropolitan University

Schooling has always tried to produce literacy in crude and mechanistic ways. Greek children learned the alphabet backwards and forwards until mastery was achieved and then set about learning the next bits backwards and forwards, and so on. The 'spellers', the basic books of literacy for two hundred years from the seventeenth to the nineteenth century, proceeded in a roughly similar way but without the 'going backwards' (although inspectors' reports from the nineteenth century did reveal children chanting forwards and backwards). These and other approaches were dominated by the need to control the literacy learning process for, as almost all educationalists believed, children were incapable of using their knowledge to act in literate ways. As Brinsley put it in 1612, if children relied too much at first on their own 'invention in making Epistles, Theames, Verses, disputing' then the resultant work will be 'nothing but froth, childishnesse and uncertaintie' (Brinsley, Ludus *literarius*). Of course, the ostensible principle of these approaches which dominated literacy education for so long was simplification, reducing the complexity of the learning task to something that could be tackled in small, comprehensible and manageable doses.

> These exercises may seem trivial at first; but as they progress, step by step, in the subsequent books of the series, to a higher and higher plane of advancement, it is believed that they will be found of very great value in advancing the pupil's knowledge of language, and his facility in the correct use of it. (Lippincott's *First Reader*, 1881)

Simplification is a very maternalistic notion. It guards against the poor young things being overwhelmed by material they cannot comprehend:

The scholarly authors of several series of readers .... have found it difficult to bring their trained minds and rich vocabularies down to the crude intellect and few lisping words of a five-year-old child. (*The Beginning Readers*, 1894)

On one level that seems fine. The tasks are simpler and easier to learn, and the tasks are easier to teach and manage. It seems that a helpful circularity has been achieved. However, on another level something has suffered and that is literacy itself. In order to be managed for learning, literacy had to be transformed. Unfortunately, the more one tried to disguise the complexity and dynamism of literacy as a social practice, and the more the curriculum was distorted to force literacy into arbitrary, manageable segments, then the greater became the distance between the schooling of literacy and its use by people in their lives outside schooling. In order to be learned, literacy had to become a different kind of object; one which had characteristics related to the pedagogical process rather than the processes of acting as literate people. A metamorphosis theory of learning dominated the teaching of literacy; before one could act as a literate person, one had go through the larval stage of achieving mastery of basic skills:

Do not under any circumstances place the book in the hands of the pupil until the foundation work has been thoroughly mastered. (*New Education Readers*: Primer, 1900)

History can show us that 'basics' have almost always been defined in terms of decontextualised skills that will one day lead to a magical metamorphosis into perfect readers and writers. History also shows us that often it did not happen. While children were being subjected to these processes, the very last thing they were to be allowed to do was to use their knowledge to act as literate people, or to use their understanding of literacy in ways that meant something. School notions of literacy were incredibly powerful and coercive and a consequence of the above circularity was that the product of management process came to define formally what was to count as literacy. Thus the real use of literacy became distanced from the learning of literacy, despite the avowed intent of literacy-teaching being to produce people who could use their literacy outside and beyond school. Practice in using literacy lost out in the squash of learning through manageable exercises.

It seems that as we move towards a new millennium so the principles of the past are being resurrected. Is the future of literacy education to be one in which the literacy curriculum is written by anonymous people who believe that arbitrariness is a necessary price to pay for successful management; one in which the pacing, sequence and control of learning is determined by authorities who have never met the children being taught; one in which complex social uses of literacy that are not easily measured are expelled to the outer reaches of the pedagogical universe because they don't fit within the ideological orbit of the literacy hour; one in which principles and justifications are unexplored and practices simply exist as clusters of discrete objects in government documents; one in which practices are based less on research and more on the imagination of groups of people sitting around in committee rooms; one in which differentiation becomes a redundant concept as the implicit redefinition of children as uniform products means that they can be subjected to assembly line principles in which teachers are reduced to being mere technicians; one in which the 'exercise' will once more define the nature of literacy; and one in which people who point out limitations, contradictions and absences are construed as 'not caring about standards'.

Most of all, are we to forget why, in the seventies and eighties, so many teachers reacted against the stultifying experiences that were being fed to children, and viewed so excitedly practices which enabled them to witness for the first time children enthusiastically embracing literacy as a complex object and using it as a powerful social tool in the classroom. The literacy agendas of that period may not have been perfect but they brought into focus elements which had been missing from all previous literacy education.

If we are not simply to recreate another version of the past, then certain new understandings about literacy must not be marginalised, written out of documents, avoided because they are less easily measured, or given less status than 'exercises'.

A strategy for literacy education that fails to:

- recognise the dynamic complexity of literacy

- recognise that the dynamic complexity is a function of the ideological and contextualised nature of literacy; in other words – its 'real-worldness'

- accept that complexity is not something to be hidden from children but something they should be encouraged to explore

- provide children from the start with experiences which allow them to act as people who need to, and can, use literacy to act upon the world as they experience it

is a literacy curriculum that looks backwards rather than forwards. The evidence of recent years shows that even the youngest children can function in literate ways, using their knowledge and skills to act upon the world. To deny them them the opportunity to do so would be a negative and regressive.

It is commonly thought that a child has not really learnt anything until it can repeat the alphabet, spell words, and read short sentences. All this has almost always been accomplished at the cost of many tears and much grief to the poor child. (*The mother's primer*, 1844)

7

Achieving Key Goals

Peter Hannon

Division of Education, University of Sheffield

A strategic agenda for literacy depends on understanding our current situation, identifying key goals and finding the methods most likely to achieve them.

The current situation

There *is* a literacy problem in this country. The ability to use written language is as vital as ever to learning, a productive life, and full citizenship. In education it remains central at every stage from reception class to FE or HE. The problem is not at the upper end of the achievement range where there are many effective and confident users of written language but in the huge variation in achievement and the 'long tail' at the lower end. There are too many children whose restricted literacy denies them access to the curriculum and who leave school with minimal qualifications. They enter a society with 'no place to hide' in using written language. Too many adults have literacy difficulties which prevent them finding employment or re-training for new jobs.

A national strategy has further problems. Many teachers and tutors, vital for policies to raise literacy, are de-motivated, under-valued, and de-skilled by current policy. Educational policy has been driven by a distrust of professionals and an emphasis on teacher-proof solutions which by-pass teachers' thinking. Opportunities for professional development are restricted to training in how to implement centrally determined programmes. Teachers and tutors struggle with a shortage of resources – textbooks, school libraries and public libraries

We are also in a confusing period of rapid, technologically-driven change. 'On-screen literacy' requires altered reading and writing skills and is

33

opening up new ways in which written language can satisfy basic communicative and expressive purposes. 'Print literacy', too, is being changed by technology – particularly in the interrelationships between image and word. There will be implications for how we conceptualise and measure achievement and under-achievement in literacy.

Another feature of the current situation – evidenced by this publication – is that literacy has become an ideological battleground. For example, saying that workforce literacy levels are too low for international economic competitiveness is both a claim about literacy and a claim about determinants of national economic performance – in particular about the causes of unemployment. Such claims may be intended to direct attention away from other economic factors such as investment policies, employers' needs for a pool of unemployed workers, low public expenditure on education, and so on. Also, the adverse effects of persistent poverty or family unemployment on educational achievement are not problems which can be tackled only by changing the teaching of literacy. Many groups have an interest in certain ways of framing, exaggerating or minimising problems or in urging certain solutions. All claims about the current literacy problem therefore have to be read critically.

We must not overlook positive features in the current situation. They include: the high level of interest in literacy, across a wide range of groups; this country still being one of the most literate in the world; increasing multilingualism; and most citizens being native speakers of one of the most widely-used languages.

Key goals

I urge four priorities for the next five years.

- **Reduce low achievement in primary education**. This phase must be the priority since the longer children are allowed to fall behind, the harder it is for them to catch up, and the greater the waste of resources. Raise overall levels of achievement by reducing the 'tail'. Action can be before school entry and in the early years of schooling

- **Develop an effective range of 'sweeping up' programmes.** These are needed at all stages to enable children falling behind to be identified and helped. Reading Recovery is only one example; there need to be many more, targeted at different categories of learners at different ages

- **Expand 'return to learning' choices.** These are needed for the many who have already left school and for those beyond the reach of programmes in the school years. Choice means literacy learning opportunities available in different settings – workplace, community, FE – for different ethnic and age groups

- **Integrate research into policy formation.** Research can enable us to refine methods and obtain better value for money from different programmes. We need more than prejudice, fashion and ideology to develop effective policy.

Means for achieving goals

Here are a dozen suggestions to assist progress towards goals.

- Increase resourcing per pupil in primary education to level of secondary. Use the extra for literacy

- Develop a *range* of remedial approaches. Do not rely on 'one shot' solutions

- Change funding arrangements for adult education and FE to encourage provision of a wider range of post-school literacy learning opportunities

- Energise teachers – make them part of the solution, not part of the problem. Trust them. Restore autonomy. Improve professional development opportunities. End the search for 'teacher-proof' programmes

- Involve parents. Start early. Recognise more than one model of family literacy

- Increase local responsibility, decrease central control

- Do not duck the resources issues. Even if government cannot increase resources immediately, it should end the pretence that there is no problem. This is especially important in compensatory programmes

- Be open to new forms of literacy. Do not try to resist the tide of new technology re-defining what it means to be literate

- Get back to basics, of which the most fundamental are learners understanding what purposes written language can serve for them and how they can acquire it. Focus on skills but never to the exclusion of purposes. Keep in mind the fundamental purposes of education. Foster critical literacy from the start

- Establish literacy as a main strand of a national educational research programme. Use central government funds to stimulate/steer a national research strategy in partnership with universities, LEAs, ESRC, EU, etc. Allocate a reasonable proportion of expenditure for evaluation (2% for established provision, 10-20% for innovations). Stick at research questions until they are solved (not just for predetermined periods of time). Use longitudinal studies. Go beyond simple 'it works' studies to comparisons of alternatives. Ensure evaluation findings shape next stage of strategy

- Resist temptation to present non-literacy problems as literacy problems

- Think long term. Have a sense of urgency but act as if there is a future beyond the next parliamentary session. End cynical, short term PR gimmicks.

Where to start?

The next government should start by saying, 'There is a literacy problem. We haven't got all the answers but we are going to mobilise people to tackle it.' Government should take some initiatives centrally but concentrate on returning responsibility – and accountability – to those who have to implement solutions, and give them the tools to do the job.

8
Reading Recovery – a Lifeline for Some

Angela Hobsbaum

Reading Recovery National Network, Institute of Education, University of London

Everyone agrees that 'prevention is better than cure', but when it comes to preventing reading problems, there is a noticeable lack of will to make prevention a real possibility for all those children who need it.

Reading Recovery prevents children who are experiencing literacy difficulties after one year at school from slipping further behind until their reading and writing difficulties undermine their learning across the whole curriculum. It achieves this by providing help for children aged around six and its success rests on a number of features which have been fully described elsewhere (Clay, 1992, 1993; Hurry, 1996).

What can Reading Recovery do for reading in the UK?

There has been much debate recently about general standards of literacy and about Britain's place in the international literacy league tables, but one point of consensus emerges: there is a 'long tail of under- achieve- ment'. This was noted by Brooks, Pugh and Schagen (1996) in their survey of 9 year olds, and by the survey into reading standards in three London authorities carried out by OFSTED (1996). It is also generally recognised that early identification and remediation are essential if literacy difficulties are to be overcome before they become entrenched. Reading Recovery provides such an early intervention system.

- **It is targeted** at children of about 6, who have had one year to adjust to the demands of school, but who are already falling behind their classmates

- **Through sensitive and informative screening**, it detects the lowest-achieving children, who are selected to receive the programme first. They would otherwise demand the most attention from the class teacher as she struggles to bridge the gap between those whose reading is leaping ahead and those getting left even further behind

- **It provides an effective programme** to enable them to reach at least the average of their class, and to develop a secure literacy system, which will be 'self-extending' because they will know how to learn and how to tackle new challenges in reading and writing

- **The teacher constantly reviews children's progress** to ensure that as soon as they are nearing their goal of literacy achievement, their programme will be aligned more closely with the classroom curriculum to enable a smooth transition as the child becomes an independent reader and writer

- **It doesn't waste resources** but makes them available to the very lowest-achieving children, only for as long as they are needed. If it becomes clear that the child is not making the progress which will be required to become an independent reader/writer, the teacher will instigate a further process of review, alerting the school to the fact that a different kind of long-term specialist help is needed

- **Reading Recovery does not aim to improve reading standards generally**; it focuses on the children at the end of the 'long tail', at the 10-20% of lowest achievers, in order to accelerate their learning so they catch up before they fall too far behind. The impact on the class or school average is variable, but the lowest achievers are those who, if their needs are not addressed in time, are likely to become the most expensive drain on the system's resources. Long-term specialist help, special schooling and school failure are not cheap solutions. The cost to society of a semi-literate underclass is immense.

Who benefits from Reading Recovery?

- The testimony of many teachers attests to the value of the Reading Recovery training course. '*I found the whole course stimulating and rewarding; it was perhaps one of the most difficult courses I have*

*attended throughout my teaching career because it was so intensive.'
'I found the structure and method of my training absolutely excellent.'
'I began my Reading Recovery training with a healthy scepticism; I
am now a total convert!' 'I have learnt a great deal about how
children learn to read and write and have been able to take back to
my teaching workable and effective practices.'*

- The children who are tutored clearly benefit also. Their parents
notice: *'although he isn't 'top of the class', S. has achieved a lot, he
is no longer withdrawn and unconfident and the other night, when
his two-year-old brother had trouble going to sleep, he read him two
Postman Pat stories; that could not have happened without Reading
Recovery.' 'K now picks up books and tries to read every word when
before she just looked at the pictures and tried to guess what the story
was.' 'J. has generally become more confident; her attitude towards
books has changed quite considerably.' 'He reads to his younger
sister and they both enjoy it.'*

But the gains are wider than merely teacher and pupils. If the Reading
Recovery teacher is also a class teacher, the evidence is that she will use
her enhanced understanding in the wider arena of her class; she will know
how to organise her book resources most effectively and how to match
children's reading needs to the most appropriate texts, and this will benefit the whole class. About one quarter of all Reading Recovery teachers
in the UK work as class teachers, sharing their class with another teacher
for part of each day.

A further 50% of all Reading Recovery teachers provide learning support
for pupils across the school. Here too, Reading Recovery teachers can
make good use of their expertise to help older pupils and those who need
less intensive support. The Reading Recovery teacher will also be able to
establish clear and effective monitoring procedures within the school, a
fact often commended in OFSTED inspections. Recent examples
include: *'There is good support for pupils who find reading difficult. The
Reading Recovery programme has made an outstanding contribution'.
'Planning and recording systems are now well established. Practice has
been influenced significantly by recent Reading Recovery Inset.'*

The school where a Reading Recovery teacher works can pride itself on having a very special expert: a teacher who knows about early literacy learning and how to foster and support it. The Reading Recovery teacher can be an asset to colleagues, advising on the organisation and purchase of resources, monitoring the progress of any children giving concern, and working with colleagues to meet their needs almost before problems arise.

The local authority which employs a Reading Recovery tutor gains an expert in early literacy and professional development, who will train Reading Recovery teachers and provide ongoing support for them through inservice courses.

Helping schools to help themselves

Under the Code of Practice for children with special educational needs (DFEE, 1994), the initial responsibility for helping children with learning difficulties rests squarely with the school. Reading Recovery provides an effective school-based early intervention which reduces the need for further help and enables the specialist psychological services to focus on particularly intractable cases. Many educational psychologists now realise that a child who has not made progress in Reading Recovery clearly needs additional long-term support and ensure that the statement of special needs is processed without delay.

How well does Reading Recovery work in the UK?

The latest figures (Hobsbaum, 1996) show that about 80% of children who receive the programme make tremendous gains and after 20 weeks are able to tackle the challenges of reading and writing as capable learners. Only one child in five of the very lowest achievers will need ongoing literacy support. These figures suggest that, where it is available, Reading Recovery can significantly reduce the 'long tail of low achievement'.

A Reading Recovery teacher in every school: an affordable dream?

Five years after it was first introduced to the UK, Reading Recovery now operates in 28 local educational authorities, with more joining every year. About 5,000 children received the programme last year, about 1% of all 6 year olds. It is estimated that 15-20% of the age group could benefit from the programme, and, in some areas, this might require more than one Reading Recovery teacher per primary school. There are about 18,000 primary schools in the country, and at present fewer than 1,000 Reading Recovery teachers. To bring the safety net of Reading Recovery within reach of every 6 year old who needs it would require a sustained teacher-training programme and could not be achieved overnight. Given the current resources, it would take five years to train a tutor for every local education authority, and ten years for them to train enough teachers for every primary school. Such a sustained investment in skilled human resources would not be cheap.

But the price of ignoring the problem is not cheap. It has been estimated that the cost of a statement of special educational needs is £3,000 just for the administrative procedures alone; the cost of providing assistance may be ten times higher. In the long term, early intervention is a cost-effective solution. Reading Recovery offers a well-integrated intervention system which has shown itself, in the last five years, capable of helping Britain's weakest readers. Can we afford to ignore their needs?

References

Brooks G, Pugh A K and Schagen I (1996) Reading Performance at Nine. Slough: NFER/Open University

Clay M M (1992) Reading Recovery: the wider implications of an educational innovation. In A Watson and A Badenhop (eds) Prevention of Reading Failure. Ashton Scholastic.

Clay M M (1993) Reading Recovery: A Guidebook for Teachers in Training. Auckland NZ: Heinemann

DFE (1994) Code of Practice on the identification and assessment of special educational needs.

Hobsbaum A, (1996) Reading Recovery in the UK. 1995/6. Unpublished report.

Hurry J (1996) What is so special about Reading Recovery'? The Curriculum Journal 7 (I) pp 93-108

9

Literacy: the Changing Landscape of Communication

Gunther Kress

Head of Culture Communication and Societies Group, Institute of Education,
University of London

The context

A strategic agenda for literacy for the next five years will need to provide the framework for practice for the two or three decades beyond that period. This agenda has to be framed in two contexts.

• The landscape of communication is undergoing a profound transformation, with far reaching effects on the place, values and forms of writing. Western societies are at the threshold of a new era of the visual

• The social and economic context in which the literacy agenda has to be considered is undergoing the most far-reaching changes since the beginning of the first industrial revolution. The effects of the globalisation of finance and of culture, are matched by a move to information-based economies.

There are further considerations, of which two must be highlighted.

• The impact of electronic technologies on information management and communication

• and the rapid development of sites of education beyond the institution of formal schooling. Without a consideration of these four factors, no clear or relevant strategy can be developed.

Below I briefly sketch a supporting argument under the following headings:

• visualisation, and its effects on writing and communication generally

* electronic information technologies and their effects on literacy practices

* social and cultural life, and new demands on knowledge of literacy

* speech and writing.

All discussions of literacy issues proceed at the moment, implicitly sometimes (calls for a return to various versions of the golden age) explicitly at other times, in terms of a common-sense about language which derives from the social and economic givens of the last century. This is a difficult item to put on the agenda; however, if we cannot change that, everything else can only be partial.

I. 'Visualisation'

The last three decades or so have been witness to a profound change in the landscape of communication in most 'Western' post-industrial societies. It is a shift of the most fundamental kind, in which written language has been displaced from its previously central position in many forms of formal public communication by the use of visual images. Some central examples of this shift are: the print-media, school textbooks, the pages of magazines, the front pages of newspapers. Where twenty five years ago the front pages even of 'tabloid' newspapers were covered in print (and were usually in black and white), a look at any example of the popular press now shows pages dominated by (large) images, where printed language is nearly pushed off the page. Textbook pages for students in the middle-years of secondary school tell the same story, whether in Geography, Biology or in Science.

'Visualisation' is one of the dominant concerns on the agenda of the IT industries. Research here is driven by a twin motivation. On the one hand by the realisation that information, visually displayed, offers massive advantages over information carried in writing. It is easier to organise, display and to take in very large quantities of information of certain kinds through the medium of a visual display than through its equivalent in written language. On the other hand, the increasing availability of 'bandwidth' now makes 'visualisation' possible and attractive for vast tracts of the informational economy. This is not to mention the needs of the producers of 'bandwidth' to find markets for their newly abundant commodity.

At the moment it is impossible to know what the end point of this process will be, and where the new equilibrium will be. It is important to keep a clear view of this process. Writing will not disappear; it will remain an essential form of representation and of communication: however its place in the landscape is changing and will change further. It will remain the major mode for communication by political and social élites. It is unlikely that it will remain the dominant mode in many significant social/cultural domains, as in the case of science.

One trend which is beginning to be discernible in the midst of this dynamic is an increasing informational specialisation of language and of the visual, in accordance with their deeper 'logic'. The logic of spatial display of visual communication offers different possibilities to the logic of temporal/sequential unfolding of spoken and (to a lesser extent) written language. Each also offers certain resistances: spoken language lends itself very readily to the communication of sequences of actions and events, while visual display lends itself equally readily to the communication of the relationship between salient elements in this world. It is no accident that the information needed – 'at the fingertips' – of airline pilots or forex dealers is visually displayed.

The relations between this development in 'literacy', and technological and economic developments are of the utmost significance. Here is the first item for the agenda. Developing the means for understanding these changes; developing means for utilising these changes; and changing school-curricula so that they are focused on providing essential understanding and skills in relation to these changes.

2. Electronic information technologies

Much current concern is focused on literacy and information technology, and quite correctly so. However, discussions tend, too often, to be concerned with relatively superficial aspects of this. The topics which I consider need serious thought and research are:

- the shift from (page and) book to screen

- the shift from text as an ordered world to text as a set of resources

- the shift from the ordered path of present textual forms (narrative, report, essay) to the unordered arrangement of the hypertext; and, a consequence of all of these

- a shift from reading to use.

• The book can be taken to be the medium par excellence of the high point of the era of literacy; it epitomises its practices, its values, and its prized forms of knowledge. *Reading a book* is what is now, still, seen as definitive of the fully literate person; it is the focus of much work in the early years of schooling. Reading encourages sustained concentration, analysis and reflection, a specific form of rationality. *Screens*, by contrast, provide a bounded amount of information, implicitly dictated by the size, shape and the possibilities of the screen. This is intensified by the possibility of projecting the contents of the computer screen on to large screens, thereby making the relation between me and my screen a publicly available form of communication. The reciprocally linked pro-cesses of producing the form and content for a screen, and the reading of a screen, will inevitably produce not only new practices of reading, but also new attitudes to information.

The power of the *screen* (from the screen of the film, to that of the TV/video, to the screen of the computer) has its effects on the former shapes of the high era of print-culture: the front pages of newspapers; the look of the pages in the new science text-books; and so on. There is now a dynamic inter-relation between screen, page and book, in which the book and the page imitate the screen. This will have the profoundest effects on practices of reading – not just the reading of *screens*, but all reading.

• If we take narrative as the western textual form par excellence (whether as epic, biography, story, anecdote, recollection, etc.) we have an ordered representation of the world. This is not a direct copy of the world but a construct. Its effect, however, is potent, in that we come to expect the world to have an order which reflects the order of the major textural forms of our cultures. The shift presaged by new technologies, taking hypertext as an example, is a move from this neatly established order to a set of possibilities, a web of choices. Where the narrative is entered at the beginning and is followed along the narrative line to a point of closure, the new textual resources can be entered at any point, and followed in directions of the user's choosing. That this is not, in fact, really so does not detract from the appearance of the potential of this new arrangement.

The effects of these shifts will be felt in reading practices, but above all in the possibilities of production. Potentially what opens up before the user of this technology is the possibility of unlimited new production. The new science text-book is not read from beginning to end (whereas science books of the 1930s, 40s and 50s were): it is not organised by *chapters,* but by *units of work*, which consist of one or two page layouts which are *used*, more than *read*. Even children's books, especially when they appear on the computer screen (whether as CD-ROM or not) offer choice points and alternative outcomes: did the three little pigs go to the town or to the farmer's apple tree? and what happened in each case?

The consequence for practices of writing and reading are deeply significant. In relation to writing, present literacy curricula aim for competent use of a system of communication. The goal for a new literacy curriculum must be competence in design, that is competence in the innovative use of available resources for making meaning in relation to the designer's intentions.

This shift from competence in the use of existing means, to innovative and transformative reshaping of existing resources in accordance with the demands of the maker's design, corresponds in any case to the demands of the new information-based economics of the coming decades.

This is the second item for the strategic agenda for literacy: an exploration of present and likely future trends in electronically mediated communication; their likely effects on both the 'stuff' of literacy and on its uses (i.e. changed practices of 'reading'), and the relation of these changes to the economics of the coming decades.

3. Social and cultural life

We know that our means for making meaning have deeply transforming effects on culture and on individuals. These are not mere skills; the salient textual forms of a cultural group provide models for thinking; for organising ideas and actions; for forms of social interaction. As a consequence, the shifts in the landscape of communication are not just changes in the technical/technological possibilities of communication, but involve deep changes for forms of cognition, for forms of action, and for forms of social interaction. Very little is known about this core aspect of literacy, although work has begun on this, over the last fifteen years or so (under the category of 'Genre') in the United States, in Australia, and in Canada, in the main.

This issue, as indeed in all other fields of literacy, becomes sharply focused and particularly problematic in deeply multicultural societies. All cultural groups have valued and salient forms of texts which arise out of the social and geographical histories of each group. Multicultural societies thus have a plethora of textual forms, all pointing to different possibilities cognitively, culturally and socially. These represent the greatest wealth of wisdom, information and knowledge, providing there is a requisite understanding and a political will to unlock this wealth.

In societies whose future well-being depends on deep-seated dispositions of innovation as they enter confidently – or hesitantly – into the age of information-based economics, understanding and the means for the productive use of this cognitive/cultural wealth and its potential will be a resource of unequalled value.

This represents one further item for the strategic agenda of literacy. Deeply ingrained dispositions of confident acceptance and productive use of difference, change, and, innovation will be essential. This item therefore has at least equal first place on the agenda.

The theoretical foundations on which work around literacy proceeds were laid down at the end of the last and the beginning of this century. These were apt for the needs of nineteenth century western European societies, and for the dominant forms of the economy of that time. In these theories societies are rigid entities; language is a system of categories and rules sustained by norm and convention. Even from the present perspective these theories look increasingly inappropriate: they are simply unusable as a basis both for the societies and the forms of economies of the next decades.

Hence the item without which not much progress is possible on any part of the strategic agenda, is a fundamental rethinking of our theories about meaning and communication. Present theories are theories of competent use in which individuals are sustained and constrained by the force of convention. Apt new theories will be theories of the transformative and innovative action by individuals.

4. Speech and writing

The two major forms in which language is manifested are speech and writing. Mainstream linguistics has laboured to produce knowledge of language as an abstractly conceived system. As a result we have very little knowledge of the 'stuff' of either speech or writing. This situation has begun to be remedied, perhaps from the early 1980s onward, but it remains the case that we do not know enough either *about language as writing or about language as speech.*

Spoken language will continue to remain the dominant mode of communication (in terms of frequency of use, etc.) for the foreseeable future. Written language will continue to remain the dominant form of communication for certain of the élites in societies. That fact alone makes it essential that efforts are intensified to provide adequate descriptions of the characteristics of written forms of language, and their difference from the characteristics of speech (therefore an urgent field of research too), and the dynamic interactions between both models, set in a full context of their social uses. All this makes it essential to provide all means necessary for full access to this form of communication for all members of society. It is one of the major paradoxes of this period that despite a century's work in linguistics, we do not have the knowledge required to provide fully explicit curricula for spoken and written English: whether for schools, teacher education, and, increasingly important, for much of literacy education outside formal schooling. Nor do we have, as a consequence, either a large group of people capable of providing inservice or professional development, or the materials for those who need to have this knowledge. That much is obvious. That the obvious needs to be stated points to a major problem.

A five point strategic literacy agenda

- investigation of the characteristics of the changes in the landscape of communication; of the new specialisation of language and image; and of the new place and valuation of language

- investigation of deep changes to literacy practices – writing and reading – by different forms of electronic technologies

- investigation of the literacy resources of multi-cultural societies; and of the potentials of bringing all into productive use

- development of theories of language, literacy and communication, appropriate to the needs of the economies of the coming decades

- development of full descriptions of the characteristics of spoken and written language; development of explicit curricula for all sites of literacy education; and provision of materials, training and development in these curricula for all literacy professionals, as needed.

10

Letter to the Minister

Jane Mace

Department of Educational Studies, Goldsmiths College, University of London

Dear Secretary of State for Education

I am writing to tell you why, in the task of building a literate nation, it is essential for you to make literacy education for the adult population a priority. I want to persuade you that, far from being the last item on your agenda, it should be the first.

Before you dismiss this as an ill-considered outburst of an eccentric, let me immediately add a couple of points. I support the view that funding for literacy in the early years is absolutely vital. I believe, too, that the rich array of initiatives in primary and secondary literacy also needs to be celebrated and funded generously. Scandalously under-funded nurseries, schools (and the university departments which train their staff) deserve your most urgent attention.

At first sight, however, it might seem that my case for adult literacy education is intended to subtract funds and policy support from these sectors of education. It is not. It is intended, instead, to persuade you that no statutory programme of literacy education can ever be complete unless it takes for granted the recognition that literacy is a lifelong experience.

Literacy in life is about *franchise*, in the fullest sense of the word. As you know, franchise is about the right of voting at public elections. It is also about freedom, of two kinds: freedom from subjection and the freedom of a 'body corporate or politic'. Less familiar might be a further sense of franchise, a characteristic of individuals and collectives of critical importance to our social and cultural health expressed as 'nobility of mind: liberality, magnanimity'.[1] In today's global economies and national or local cultures, literacy – the medium of expression and communication between people via reading and writing – represents a most potent means to exercise freedom and give expression to individual and collective magnanimity.

Let me paint you a picture. It is a scene repeated up and down the country of a particular transaction between state and citizen. The literacy 'moment' in it – the moment when the official passes the form to the individual and the individual reacts to it – concerns a relationship of power between one and the other. In sketching people into the scene, I have deliberately omitted any suggestion of what their gender, age, ability, ethnic identity might be: because I want to strip to the minimum the possibility for quibble in the question I want to ask you. The question is this:

'Of all the people in this scene and the invisible ones beyond it, which do you think are the person or persons who could benefit from a programme of adult literacy education?'

We are in a government office.

> (It does not matter, for the argument, what kind of office. It could be designed for people to claim state benefits, to register as unemployed, to seek asylum.)

There is a queue. People have been waiting a long time. The person at the head of the queue is facing a government official.

The official is holding a form, which the person needs to complete in writing.

> (Unseen, but present elsewhere in the same building, are other officials, in offices. Beyond, in council chambers and the House of Commons, are the elected representatives of the people).

The person at the head of the queue exhibits difficulty with doing this. Maybe they ask if they can take the form home. Or maybe they ask the official to help them.

The other people in the queue are tired. It is raining. There is an impatience in the air.

The positive case for a literate life stands in direct contrast with the case for literacy as a problem. The idea of a 'crisis' of illiteracy in industrialised countries in the 1970s which constructed the response to be a remedial service still dominates too much policy thinking. I suggest that it may still be dominating yours. According to this idea, the government only has to 'do something about it' ('it' being adult literacy), not because it is an obvious and essential part of education to consider, but because there is a perceived 'gap' in skills necessary to our economy revealed by the latest survey sitting on your desk. Now, if where you start from is crises and gaps, it is understandable that you think in terms of fixes and remedies. Understandable too is the arrival of a rather sad expression in the public debates: the phrase 'preventive literacy'. (The association is with preventive medicine. The assumption it carries is that literacy is the fix for illiteracy).

The case I want to put to you starts from a different position: a position which says that it is not individual remediation which is needed, but a change in the culture; and that it is not merely the individual having difficulty with the government form who 'needs' or should have the opportunity of adult literacy education, but all the other people involved in the scene. For a nation to become fully literate, funds – and thinking – need to be allocated to what being literate means. I am not suggesting a semantic debate about definitions (although that is always a good exercise). I am suggesting, instead, what teacher educators know is essential for any teachers to be effective: some honest reflection. In short, the adult literacy education to which you need to give priority is an educational enterprise which engages all of us, not just a strange and alarming minority seen to be deficient.

Both you and I (and very possibly the reader of this book) operate in writing factories – reading and writing from morning to night. Both university education (which currently employs me) and government business (in which you work) are structures committed to constant reading and writing – with consequent dangers of 'information overload' for both of us. We have become ignorant of any other way of behaving. All the more urgent, then, if we are to achieve the franchise of a fully literate nation, with freedom from oppression, freedom for communities, and the opportunity for people to give voice to their nobility of mind, that we question our assumptions, and re-examine what it is that we think is so special about literacy.

I know, of course, that few people call the current provision for adults in colleges, prisons, community centres, workplaces, and school parents' rooms 'adult literacy education'. From the 1970s' campaign 'against adult illiteracy', through the 1980s developments in 'adult basic education' (extended to include numeracy and English for speakers of other languages), educational provision in this area today appears in the guise of 'skills' and support'. There are basic skills, communication skills and core skills; and then there is learning support, language support and additional support (note how that work 'support' implies language and literacy to be adjuncts to the main business of life). As you read this, all sorts of adult groups around the country are engaged in this work; in discussions about punctuation, vocabulary, spelling patterns, varieties of English, register, voice and style; interpreting street directories, NVQ elements of competence, poems, composing responses to job seeker allowance forms, letters and to life itself.

Let us return to the person in the queue. Let us, for the sake of argument, see her as a woman, in her forties, who is black; and let us now visit her in one of these settings. This time, the question I invite you to consider as you picture the scene is this:

What does your own franchise have to do with that of the people in this scene?

In the group, we had some laughs, she says. And I never thought I would be able to use the library and find things out. But our tutor got us to do some research. And we talked about it. What I have learned from that is how my story fits in a bigger one. I have still got a lot to learn. But I feel free now. Free to ask. Free to insist. Free to learn. And I am proud of my history.

We are in a classroom. There are paper cups, bottles of juice and wine, and home-made food on plates. This is a celebration. The people in the room are sharing a sense of achievement. the woman is now reading to them, haltingly, but proudly. The story she reads is of her arrival in this country. She tells the group how she wrote it. It was hard, she said. She had thought she could not write anything. Her tutor made them all work at it, though.

There is applause.

In the classroom, where this woman has been joining others each week, she had learned to voice the questions in her head as well as learning 'how to read and write'. In the classroom, the varied voices and literacy lives of others have come into play. In the classroom, all the knowledge and experience she'd forgotten she possessed in the queue in the government office, she remembers again; and she remembers that she is entitled to ask and to insist. The woman in the queue is also the woman in the classroom and many other settings. Her capacity to fulfil her rights to franchise is conditioned by the education (or lack of it) of other people in her life – including the government minister.

In the classroom, too, the other learners include the teacher, having to explore with new eyes the assumptions of a literate culture about literacy. In other settings, this teacher still finds these assumptions alive and well. Any time in conversation she reveals what her job is, that conversation is likely to continue with a listener commenting, sympathetically: 'It must be awful. I can't imagine not being able to read and write. How do they cope? How do they manage?'

Let me invite you, Minister, to ask yourself the same question, in reverse. How is it that we manage – we who are so dependent on a life of reading and writing for our sense of identity and community? What is so important about the experience of a confident and self-critical literate person? And what is it that our literacy excludes us from? The adult literacy education necessary for you, for me, for the functionary in the office and for all of us is that which recognises how the inner life of reading and writing connects each of us to a society in which there is franchise for everyone. As Rita Dove said of poetry, literacy in adult life provides 'stepping stones across the river, so we can better sense the depths'[2]

Words on the page stand as symbols of our understanding. Our very signatures symbolise more than they seem. Like the woman at the counter, you and I have first to read and assess the significance of the document in front of us before we decide whether to sign it; we must interpret the intention of those who wrote it (if it is not ourselves) and decide the wording of our response. Our signature, that deceptively simple measure of our literacy, stands as a symbol of our ability to do these things. Just as your signature every day of the week symbolises your agreement and authority, so does hers. Not only can both of you write your names, but you can read or write critically the text which precedes it and not only can you write your name, but you can do it the same way each time you do so, and in such a way that no-one else should be able to reproduce it. The signature, of all that we write, is our own utterly individual mark: whether at the end of international treaties or autograph books, housing-benefit forms or letters to ministers, the signature represents our identity both as separate individuals and as representatives of a larger community.

I have sketched one woman in two places. The argument I have been making is that the adult literacy education that is necessary to build a literate nation is that which makes a connection between them. My message to you, Minister, is that literacy is about life beyond as well as within the walls of bureaucracies and school buildings; it is about franchise in the sense that I have put it to you. In preparing this letter I have exercised my literacy abilities as well as I can – talking to others, reading all kinds of things which my inspire me, and struggling with composition. In ending it, I sign my own name – as illegibly and as uniquely as possible.

References

(1) Onions (1959) *The shorter Oxford dictionary*, Oxford University Press p.746

(2) Rita Dove, *Poetry International Lecture*, Festival Hall, London: 27.10.96

11

Enhancing the Effectiveness of Primary School Teachers

Peter D. Pumfrey

School of Education, University of Manchester

Introduction

This article deliberately restricts its focus to qualified and experienced primary school teachers. Quantitatively and qualitatively, they represent the major source of expertise capable of increasing the reservoir of effective practice within the educational system. How, over the next five years, can this group be helped to improve their own professionalism and that of their less experienced colleagues, in enhancing pupils' acquisition and enjoyment of literacy?

To any government, assertions headlined 'Literacy standards have fallen' or 'Literacy standards are lower than expected' are seen as potential political disasters. They arouse public interest and concern equivalent to 'The 'Titanic' has sunk'. Whereas the facts underpinning the latter headline were irrefutable, those underpinning the former are far less clearcut. The failure to make explicit the assumptions underpinning the standards of literacy that are **expected** of primary school pupils and the **validity** of the assessment techniques on which **judgments** about standards are based, point to the dangers of unjustified generalisations.

Over the last nine years there has been an educational revolution. We now have an explicit national educational policy and a National Curriculum. In that curriculum, English is recognised as one of three core subjects. Programmes of Study and Attainment Targets are specified. In the Primary School, Standard Assessment Tasks and Teacher Assessments are used to monitor standards and progress at the end of Key Stages 1 and 2 (NCY2 and NCY6). League Tables of the average attainments of schools in English (and other subjects) are published. Baseline assessments of children's skills on entry to school are in train. 'Value-added' comparisons between schools are being (controversially) developed. The identification, assessment, and the principles underpinning the education of children with special educational needs, including those with literacy difficulties, are provided by the Code of Practice on the Identification and Assessment of Special Educational Needs and its associated legislation. Schools are now managed by Governors with responsibility for the efficient running of the establishment and the bulk of its finances. The Office of Standards in Education (OFSTED) regularly and systematically inspects schools. Teachers are rated for their competence. The intention of such arrangements is to raise educational standards and to make schools more accountable to the clientele they exist to serve.

Challenges

It is often overlooked that accountability involves reciprocities between policy-making politicians, the professionals charged with implementing policies, parents and pupils. We now have what is called 'an entitlement curriculum'. When the balance between educational 'rights' asserted and 'responsibilities' accepted by the parties involved favours the former, teachers frequently suffer. In primary schools significant numbers of able and experienced staff are seeking early retirement. The pressures on teachers created by the number and rate of educational changes and their associated bureaucratic demands, are not conducive to effective teaching. Reducing such pressures would be one major constructive approach towards retaining, disseminating and developing the expertise such professionals have acquired.

Despite (or because of) the innovations in the state educational system outlined earlier, concern is still expressed about standards of literacy. One current concern is with what is called 'the long tail of underachievers' in literacy. Another is an apparent poor national ranking in international comparative studies of attainments. Tensions exist between the standards of literacy that social policy requires that pupils achieve in our primary schools, and the manifold differences that comprise the uniqueness of the child. Teachers are expected to be sensitive to the interests and abilities of the individual, and to value that individuality. At the same time, societal demands for conformity exist. Typically, parents expect that their children should become literate at roughly the same time. Evidence from both everyday life and from science, confirms the existence of massive differences between children in virtually any aspect of literacy. Children do not all learn to become literate in either the same way or at the same rates. This is not to say that standards and progress cannot be improved.

What actions could be taken during the next five years to help build a more literate nation?

One point is certain. There are no 'quick fixes'; no pedagogic panaceas; no 'soundbite-solutions'.

Building a literate nation

To address the concern posed by this report, we must consider the question 'What do we understand by the term 'literacy''?

According to 'The Literacy Dictionary: The Vocabulary of Reading and Writing', published by the International Reading Association, there are many difficulties in agreeing a common definition of 'literacy' (Harris and Hodges, 1995).

It is essential thus to distinguish between three levels at which the term is used.

Literacy A refers to an abstraction. As such, it cannot be directly observed or measured. The concept encapsulates the essence of the activity. Concepts are essential in seeking how to describe, predict and control the development of literacy.

Literacy B refers to the observable behaviours in everyday life from which the existence of the concept Literacy A is inferred.

Literacy C represents tests and assessment techniques that systematically sample manifestations of the concept in everyday life.

The classroom, the school, the home and the community are major arenas in which children develop and use their literacy skills. It is mainly in the first two of these that teachers observe the production of the myriad literacy-related activities of their pupils. This is not to deny the importance of the other two.

To build a literate nation demands that we understand the nature of literacy and its development in particular multicultural contexts. Literacy is one aspect of communicative abilities. Communication can be achieved either verbally or non-verbally. Communication itself is but one facet of child development.

Literacy is learned and taught over time. Child development from birth to maturity requires an understanding of the interplay between nature and nurture. Specialists from many disciplines have distinctive yet complementary contributions to make. Traditionally, in our culture, literacy comprises the ability to transmit and receive thoughts and feelings expressed through textual genres covering the many fields that comprise knowledge.

Put simply, being literate means being able to read, write and spell. Literacy builds on oracy. The receptive skills of listening and reading are coupled with the expressive ones of speaking and writing (including spelling).

In essence, literacy involves semiotic processes. The acquisition and effective application of the skills of literacy involve thinking. Literacy is both an amplifier and a consequence of the development of human abilities in a society which values the cultural and economic benefits to the individual and the group that literacy can provide. Learning to read and write is reciprocated by reading and writing to learn. In summary, literacy empowers; illiteracy impoverishes.

Semiotics has been defined as a general philosophy of communication. Many semiotic systems have been invented using notations other than the alphabet. These include computing languages, mathematics, music, architecture and art. Thus the concept of literacy is nowadays frequently qualified to indicate specific fields. For example, 'Computer literacy' is a term already in common use.

Research, literacy and professional development

Looking outwards, astrophysicists are exploring the origins of the universe. Looking inwards, the Human Genome Project is an international endeavour to map the complexities of the human genetic code. Conceptualising, operationally defining, predicting and enhancing the development of literacy is, at the very least, an equally challenging responsibility.

Advances in all these fields demand research. In education, the community, the classroom and the clinic are the 'laboratories' within which such research takes place. Teachers' awareness of the nature and applications of educational research into the 'within child' attributes, the environmental conditions that affect the acquisition of literacy, and their interactions across time in relation to the learning and teaching of literacy, are areas of professional expertise and of national importance.

Collectively, a great deal is known by various groups of professionals about conditions and contexts that encourage literacy. So are those that discourage literacy. The extension and dissemination of such understandings are continuing challenges. By encouraging systematically the 'Continuing Professional Development' of teachers within the context of a School Development Plan, these challenges can be met. A central thrust should be to encourage classroom-based research by class teachers and schools. How might this be done?

- Teachers require time to consider the pedagogic justification and implications of the National Curriculum in general and National Curriculum English in particular. Knowing 'what' to do to enhance children's literacy is a necessary **but not sufficient** condition for being a confident teacher with high professional self-esteem. An understanding of 'why' certain approaches are effective (or otherwise) with particular groups of pupils at given stages in their education, is essential. Quality time for teachers to reflect on their individual and collective professional experiences, is required

- Teachers merit sabbatical periods out of school, to reflect on their individual and collective experiences concerning children's acquisition of literacy

- The development of literacy is but one aspect of child development. Concern about the cognitive/intellectual bases of literacy must be balanced by attention to affective, social and motivational factors if both standards and progress are to be improved and the pleasures of literacy appreciated by pupils

- Teachers' expertise in the use of formative and summative assessment has been stimulated by the introduction of SATs. Despite this, there is still a paucity of experience and expertise on the uses and limitations of various modes of observation, assessment, recording and interpretation of formative and summative data. A wider integration of assessment with the learning and teaching of literacy than that based on the National Curriculum and its SATs is possible and desirable. For example, the British Psychological Society has produced materials that are designed to help non-psychologists acquire the competencies needed to use assessment techniques effectively

- Capitalise on the expertise of Literacy Co-ordinators' Special Educational Needs Co-ordinators and the class teachers within a particular school, consortia of schools, LEA, Region and nationally, by arranging courses of varying duration and at different levels on specific aspects of literacy

- Ensure that the expertise of specialists in literacy and learning (such as members of support services and educational psychologists) based outside schools, is integrated in the above programmes. Such courses should be linked to formally approved awards. Collaboration in this between the TTA and HE establishments is one promising avenue

- Every primary school teacher requires access both to computers and the opportunity of acquiring expertise

- The expansion of electronic communication networks provides an efficient means of disseminating 'good practice' or engaging in both dialogue and conference with other teachers. The ability to use e-mail is essential. Literacy improvement related networks exist. Over the next five years their use by teachers and schools can increase markedly. The opportunity exists.

Already advances in information technology enable speech to be transformed into text on a screen; spelling, syntax and semantics corrected if necessary, and printed out or communicated in speech

Increasingly, screen presentations of text will provide the information concerning issues to be considered and about which decisions must be made. Whilst conventional books will not disappear within five years, we need to look further ahead.

Work on the development of 'digital paper' is under way at the Massachusetts Institute of Technology. This 'digital paper' functions as a screen and can be presented within covers in book format, or even incorporated within a newspaper. The user selects a text from the Internet or a CD-ROM from whence the text is down-loaded directly to the page or pages until the user wishes to replace the text.

Despite the potential of IT, the effective primary school and the improvement of children's literacy will continue to be dependent on the primary school teacher.

Conclusion

Experienced and effective primary school teachers represent the main resource on which the improvement of literacy in the next five years, and in the longer term, depends. Standards of children's literacy can be enhanced. To this end, Continuing Professional Development is central.

Politicians, the Government and their employees in the DFEE, LEAs, OFSTED, SCAA and the TTA must support, rather than harangue or harass, primary school teachers in the demanding pedagogic challenges class teachers face every day with increasing numbers of pupils in their classrooms.

12

Electronic Literacy

Keith Topping

Department of Psychology, University of Dundee

'Electronic Literacy' refers to literacy activities (eg in reading, writing, spelling) which are delivered, supported, accessed or assessed through computers or other electronic means rather than on paper. It should not be confused with 'computer literacy', which refers to knowledge and competences in using computers generally. Electronic Literacy is not just an additional component to our existing definition of 'literacy', it has the potential to transform the whole definition (Tuman, 1994; Reinking, McKenna, Labbo and Kieffer, 1997).

Electronic multi-media approaches include CD-ROMs, which can offer on-screen text, static pictures, moving pictures, much faster search/ access and interactivity facilities than regular books, many alternative paths to follow from decision points, interactive questioning, suggestions for further classroom exploration, and so forth. Audiotaped books, enabling the child to read while listening, could also be considered a multi-media approach, as could videotapes.

Current developments in computer-based electronic literacy include (a) electronically supported reading, (b) electronically supported writing, (c) electronic audiences, (d) electronic literacy assessment, feedback and management, and (e) electronic direct speech-text conversion.

(a) Electronically supported reading

Much of the early commercial reading software offered little more than regular text, but on screen – less portable than a book and often more difficult to read. Some were merely worksheets or other mechanistic drill and practice tasks presented on screen rather than on paper. The relationship to research on effective pedagogy was often tenuous.

However, even a decade ago the better computer programmes were already demonstrating effectiveness in raising literacy performance in adults, let alone in children (Wangberg, 1986). Increasingly, modern adaptive computer programmes seek to scaffold and prompt successful reading (Reitsma, 1988).

Reinking and Schreiner (1985) and Reinking (1988) found that fifth and sixth grade children read text effectively from paper or screen, but adaptive software which enabled the reader to select support in the form of definitions of key vocabulary, a simpler version of the text, supplemental contextual information or an indication of the main idea for each paragraph resulted in more effective reading than either, especially on passages of high difficulty.

Salomon, Globerson and Guterman (1989) evaluated the insertion of metacognitive prompts (questions, strategies and reminders) into a simple program called The Reading Partner. The experimental group showed superior reading comprehension and essay writing. Reinking and Rickman (1990) found support for readers through definitions of key vocabulary used more by children and more effective if presented by computer rather than on paper.

The addition of voice recognition, speech synthesis and digitised speech takes the idea of electronically supported reading a stage further. Programmes now enable machines to 'hear' beginning readers and/or give individualised discriminatory prompting or corrective spoken feedback to promote oral reading accuracy (eg Moseley, 1992, Davidson and Noyes, 1994 and 1995, Hartas, 1994, Van Daal and Reitsma, 1993, Goodman, 1994).

More recently, McKenna and Watkins (1996) and McKenna (1997) described the use with beginning and disabled readers of electronic 'Talking Books' (not to be confused with the audiotaped 'Talking Books' described earlier by Carbo in 1978). Children could choose to hear digitised pronunciations of individual words. Results from this and previous studies were encouraging, suggesting that increased engagement and practice was itself a powerful factor, since the children learned many new words in addition to those for which support was accessed. It seems that such supported texts can indeed extend the child's 'zone of proximal development'. They also lend themselves to repeated readings, and meta-cognitive instruction and comprehension monitoring can be arranged in parallel as the teacher sees fit.

Examples of 'talking' reading support programs are: Wiggleworks (Scholastic), KidTalk, ULTimate Reader and Acceleread. 'Living Books' produced by Broderbund on CDROM have text and pictures with child self-selected digitised speech, second language versions, the option of playing instructional games and various special effects.

Horney and Anderson-Inman (1997) and Anderson-Inman and Horney (forthcoming) review their ElectroText program, which supports text in a wide variety of sophisticated ways. The embedded resources can be categorised as: translational (for ESL children), illustrative (including video), summarising, instructional, enrichment, notational, collaborative and general purpose. Children select the type and degree of help necessary. The authors also discuss design criteria for 'universally accessible documents'.

But what about children who are unfamiliar with keyboarding or have specific learning disabilities? The ULTimate Reader program incorporates visual highlighting as selected by the child, bilingual Spanish with customised pronunciation, different speeds and chunking of speech feedback, and auditory prompting for visually impaired users. Programs such as Computer Campus include specific keyboard skills tutorials, and enable multiple choice of screen colour, text colour, font and font size – to accommodate for any scotopic sensitivity syndrome and obviate any need to wear Irlen lenses.

(b) Electronically supported writing

The use of the regular word processor in the classroom has been shown to improve the quality of child writing (Bangert-Drowns, 1993). Beyond this, predictor programmes which also scaffold and prompt the writing process are increasingly common and increasingly sophisticated.

When the child is unsure what to write next, the machine prompts with alternatives. The computer remembers and integrates more and more about each individual child's most frequently used vocabulary, including special people and place names, as well as the child's typical constructional style. Its prompting becomes ever more attuned to the individual child's natural writing 'personality'.

Examples of current predictor programmes include: Prophet, Penfriend, Co-Writer, PAL, TextHelp, EZ Keys for Windows. Beyond this, there are programmes which prompt in speech rather than on-screen – 'talking word processors'. Examples include: Write Outloud, Textreader, Talking Textease, TalkWrite, KidWorks, Accelewrite, Talking Word for Windows, the Adult Literacy Word processor, ULTimate Reader.

Against this background, the old-fashioned word processing spell-checker begins to seem like something from the Stone Age. Modern, adaptive, prompting spell checkers do not just give the child the correct spelling, but support the child in figuring it out for him or herself (eg PAL Speller). They do not just take over the human function, but engineer effective human learning, while also enabling the child to complete the task without undue stress or sense of failure. The 'talking spell checker' is increasingly commonplace and many of the talking word processors have this inbuilt.

(c) Electronic audiences

Teachers and parents worry about kids spending hours in isolation 'playing' with their computer. However, electronic literacy can also offer children wider socialisation and an expanded view of potential audiences for their creations.

Teachers have often had children making reading books for younger ones, or to circulate among their classmates, or children writing letters and journals to peers in another school, nearby or far away. Computers enable self-made books to be produced to a far higher standard of finish.

Increasingly, children write to electronic mail pals on the other side of the world (sometimes receiving a reply or other feedback within minutes), or participate in an international exchange of news and views through an e-mail group listserver, or collaborate in producing regular issues of an electronic journal, or create material for the school's Internet world wide web homepages (Garner and Gillingham, 1996, Leu and Leu, 1997).

(d) Electronic literacy assessment, feedback and management

Computers can also assess reading. Computer-mediated texts with embedded comprehension questions, which prompt the reader to review the relevant section of text if the questions are answered incorrectly, have been evaluated (Reinking and Pickle, in press), as have multi-media book reviews (Reinking and Watkins, 1996).

Programmes for child self-assessment of silent reading comprehension of literature which give enhanced feedback are increasingly sophisticated (Paul, 1996, Paul and Topping, 1996, Vollands, Topping and Evans, 1996). The child can self-test on books read at home and school, including those read to and with the child, perhaps using the Duolog Reading technique (Topping, 1997a). In addition to providing diagnostic reports for the teacher, such software also generates take-home reports to promote parental involvement and parents might even come into school to sit in on the self-test and celebrate the outcome!

These programmes can be coupled with newly available norm-referenced (standardised) reading tests delivered, scored and interpreted by computer. Not only can such tests save a great deal of teacher time, they reduce child testing time by their adaptive nature, presenting only individually selected items to determine quickly the child's functional level. Furthermore, their large item banks mean children never take the same test twice, so they can be used repeatedly if the teacher wishes without being biased by practice effects or cheating. For children with reading difficulty, computer-based diagnostic tests designed to identify (for example) dyslexia might offer greater objectivity and consistency (Singleton, 1994). Some of these computer-based assessments also generate prescriptive advice for the teacher and the child about how to improve the performance level. For teachers interested in continuous portfolio assessment, the portfolio will increasingly be kept in electronic form (Kieffer, Hale and Templeton, 1997).

(e) Electronic direct speech-text conversion

Teaching writing in schools becomes of doubtful relevance when a computer can reliably transform speech into writing – and writing into speech. This is not a futuristic vision – the technology already exists and is in everyday use. Examples of such programs are: VoiceText with Dragon Dictate, IBM Voicetype 3 and the Phillips Text to Speech system.

One implication for schools is that teaching dictation skills might become much more important than teaching writing. The human is not redundant, but the machine performs some of the simpler functions more efficiently and thereby extends the human's capability – in other words, this is 'bionic writing'.

At the moment, programmes for Direct Speech-Text Conversion take some time to learn to discriminate the voice of specific users, so any new user has to tolerate an initial period of slow going. Also, their basic vocabulary is not large, so users need to add a good deal of their own personal vocabulary to the program lexicon. But all of this is improving rapidly. Better voice analysis and synthesis systems will enable the computer to mimic the voice of the child (or parent or whoever), rather than sounding like a mechanical stranger.

But this technology is not portable, you might be thinking. Well, actually, it is. Hand held dictation machines which convert speech direct to text are already in use (albeit largely by rich business people). When you reach a table top computer, you just extract the mini-disc from your handset, put it into the mini-drive and print, save or otherwise manipulate the file. Of course, Digital Audio Tape (DAT) recording lends itself to this process.

Access, equity and the future

These developments in software and hardware will of course be costly, at least initially. Children need to be introduced to computers in the preschool years if they are to develop capability and confidence. Wealthy schools and families will (again) be at an advantage.

Many homes have no computer, especially in areas of relative socio-economic disadvantage. Even where a computer is present in the home, the hardware platform (eg Mac, IBM, etc) and/or operating system (eg DOS, Windows, etc) might be completely different to that used in school, so programmes and files cannot be transferred. This is a particular problem in the UK, where many local education authorities have locked themselves into commitment to an idiosyncratic hardware system, while parents are (more sensibly) increasingly buying IBM clone machines for the home.

However, costly software and hardware are not effective if not used or not used well – they are a means to an end, not an end in themselves. Thus the highly motivated child who is hungry to learn may only need a small marginal increment in available technology to make substantial strides forward.

The research agenda for Electronic Literacy is substantial. Issues of effectiveness, comparative effectiveness and cost-effectiveness should be to the fore. Just because it's electronic doesn't necessarily make it better or cheaper or easier or more reliable. Continuing comparisons of cost-effectiveness with more traditional low-technology, low-cost approaches are necessary.

However, existing approaches can be extended into the electronic literacy arena, yielding new combinations which also merit exploration and evaluation. Peer Tutoring (Topping, 1988, Topping, 1995, Topping and Ehly, 1997) and Family Literacy (Wolfendale and Topping, 1996, Topping, 1997b) are prime examples.

In any event, the nature of learning (and certainly of schooling) will undoubtedly change in the face of the swelling torrent of electronic information. The traditional emphasis on detailed knowledge and retention will be replaced by more emphasis on transferable skills in selecting, processing, transforming, evaluating and adding to information – in other words, thinking. Higher order thinking skills will be increasingly in demand, and increasingly directly taught in schools. Information retained in the head will be largely 'nodal knowledge' – signposts and frameworks for navigating networks.

Electronic Literacy in the Home

There is an African proverb that it takes a whole village to raise a child. However, the traditional stereotype of a school at the centre of a village community is being replaced by the notion of a global electronic village.

Parents and children are already interacting electronically independently of the school. The National Parents' Information Network (http://ericps. ed.uiuc.edu/npin/abtnpin.html) is a project sponsored by ERIC (the Education Resources Information Centre) in the US to provide information direct to parents and those who work with parents. It also features an e-mail discussion list (Parenting-L) and a search and question answering facility – a veritable electronic guru. Teachers can now assume that parents might have access to a second opinion at the speed of electricity.

As might be expected, NPIN includes 'guidelines for helping you evaluate computer use in your child's school' – a subject on which parents can now easily be as expert as teachers. Just as some privileged children always enjoyed more frequent individualised teaching of reading at home than at school, the same is now true of learning information technology skills. Also accessible via NPIN are 'The Electronic Schoolhouse', 'Family Village', the 'Parents as Teachers National Center', 'SMART-PARENTING On-Line' and 'Keeping Kids Reading', all of which include resources for parents as educators at home, and various web sites which contain reviews of educational software by children and parents. 'Parents, Educators and Publishers' is another website of software reviews for parents and children (http://www. microweb.com/pepsite/).

Electronic magazines for families are also proliferating. 'Family World' is an electronic magazine for parents and children accessible through NPIN. 'Parents and Children Together Online' is another, in this case specifically focused on family literacy and operated by the Family Literacy Center at ERIC. Electronic contributions from children and parents are welcome! Also see Parents Place (http://www.ParentsPlace. com/). Similar developments are occurring on a smaller scale in the UK, where the Parents' Information Network (PIN) (1996) has produced 'A Parent's Guide to Computers Supporting Homework', to supplement previous guides on choosing software. And all of this is just the beginning.

Acknowledgement

Some of the work reported here was supported by the Nuffield Foundation.

References

Anderson-Inman, L. and Horney, M.A. (forthcoming) Supported Text in Electronic Reading Environments. *Reading and Writing Quarterly* (themed issue on electronic literacy).

Bangert-Drowns, R.L. (1993) The Word Processor As An Instructional Tool: A Meta-Analysis of Word Processing in Written Instruction. *Review of Educational Research* 63 (1) 1993.

Carbo, M. (1978) Teaching Reading With Talking Books. *The Reading Teacher* 32, 267-273.

Davidson, J. and Noyes, P. (1994) Computer-Generated Speech Feedback as Support for Reading Instruction. in: Singleton, C. (ed) *Computers and Dyslexia: Educational Applications of New Technology*. Department of Psychology, University of Hull.

Davidson, J. and Noyes, P. (1995) Computer-Generated Speech Feedback as Support for Reading Instruction. *Support For Learning* 10 (1) 35-39.

Garner, R. and Gillingham, M.G. (1996) *Internet Communication in Six Classrooms: Conversation Across Time, Space and Culture*. Mahwah NJ: Erlbaum.

Goodman, S. (1994) Reading Success. *Special Children* 77, 36-40.

Hartas, C. (1994) 'Say-That-Again, Please': A Reading Program Using a Speaking Computer. in: Singleton, C. (ed) *Computers and Dyslexia: Educational Applications of New Technology*. Department of Psychology, University of Hull.

Horney, M.A. and Anderson-Inman, L. (1997) Transforming Texts for At-Risk Readers. In: Reinking, D., McKenna, M., Labbo, L. and Kieffer, R.D. (eds), *Literacy for the 21st Century: Technological Transformations in a Post-Typographical World*. Mahwah NJ : Erlbaum (forthcoming).

Kieffer, R.D., Hale, M.E. and Templeton, A. (1997) Electronic Literacy Portfolios: Technology Transformations in a First Grade Classroom. In: Reinking, D., McKenna, M., Labbo, L. and Kieffer, R.D. (eds), *Literacy for the 21st Century: Technological Transformations in a Post-Typographical World*. Mahwah NJ : Erlbaum (forthcoming).

Leu, D.J. and Leu, D.D. (1997) *Teaching With the Internet: Lessons From the Classroom*. Norwood MA : Christopher-Gordon.

McKenna, M.C. (1997) *Electronic Texts and the Transformation of Beginning Reading*. In: Reinking, D., McKenna, M., Labbo, L. and Kieffer, R.D. (eds), *Literacy for the 21st Century: Technological Transformations in a Post-Typographical World*. Mahwah NJ: Erlbaum (forthcoming).

McKenna, M.C. and Watkins, J. (1996) Using Talking Books with Beginning Readers. Paper presented at International Reading Association Annual Convention, New Orleans, April 28 – May 3.

Moseley, D.V. (1992) Visual and Linguistic Determinants of Reading Fluency in Dyslexics: A Classroom Study with Speaking Computers. in: Groner, R., Kaufmann-Hayoz, P. and Wright, S.F. (eds) *Reading and Reading Disorders: International Perspectives*. Amsterdam : Elsevier.

Paul, T.D. (1996) Combining Cybernetic Theory and Information Technology to Improve Literacy Instruction and Motivation Through Feedback Enhancement: A Study of 2500 Texas Schools. Paper delivered at 'Literacy and Technology for the 21st Century' conference, National Reading Research Centre, Atlanta Georgia, October 4-5.

Paul, T.D. and Topping, K.J. (1996) Computer Assisted Assessment of Reading Practice: Variation According to Age, Reading Ability, State, School Size and School Type. Paper delivered at 'Literacy and Technology for the 21st Century' conference, National Reading Research Centre, Atlanta Georgia, October 4-5.

Reinking, D. (1988) Computer-Mediated Text and Comprehension Differences: The Role of Reading Time, Reader Preference and Estimation of Learning. *Reading Research Quarterly* 23, 484-498.

Reinking, D. and Pickle, M. (1996) The Effects of Inserted Questions and Mandatory Review in Computer-Mediated Texts. *Reading Research Quarterly* (in press)

Reinking, D. and Rickman, S.S. (1990) The Effects of Computer-Mediated Texts on the Vocabulary Learning and Comprehension of Intermediate Grade Readers. *Journal of Reading Behavior* 22 (4) 395-411.

Reinking, D. and Schreiner, R. (1985) The Effects of Computer-Mediated Text on Measures of Reading Comprehension and Reading Behavior. *Reading Research Quarterly* 20, 536-551.

Reinking, D. and Watkins, J. (1996) *A Formative Experiment Investigating the Use of Multimedia Book Reviews to Increase Elementary Students' Independent Reading*. University of Georgia and University of Maryland, National Reading Research Center.

Reinking, D., McKenna, M., Labbo, L. and Kieffer, R.D. (eds) (1997) *Literacy for the 21st Century: Technological Transformations in a Post-Typographical World*. Mahwah NJ: Erlbaum (forthcoming).

Reitsma, P. (1988) Reading Practice for Beginners: Effects of Guided Reading, Reading-While-Listening and Independent Reading with Computer-Based Speech Feedback. *Reading Research Quarterly* 23, 219-235.

Salomon, G., Globerson, T. and Guterman, E. (1989) The Computer as a Zone of Proximal Development: Internalising Reading Related Metacognitions From a Reading Partner. *Journal of Educational Psychology* 81 (4) 620-627.

Singleton, C. (1994) (ed) *Computers and Dyslexia: Educational Applications of New Technology*. Department of Psychology, University of Hull.

Topping, K.J. (1988) *The Peer Tutoring Handbook: Promoting Cooperative Learning*. London: Croom Helm; Cambridge MA : Brookline.

Topping, K.J. (1995) *Paired Reading, Writing and Spelling: The Handbook for Teachers and Parents*. London and New York : Cassell.

Topping, K.J. (1997a) *Duolog Reading: Video Training Pack*. Madison WI: Institute for Academic Excellence.

Topping, K.J. (1997b) Family Electronic Literacy. Reading (UKRA) in press)

Topping, K.J. and Ehly, S. (eds) (1997) *Peer Assisted Learning*. Mahwah NJ and Hove UK: Erlbaum.

Tuman, M. (1994) *Word Perfect: Literacy in the Computer Age*. London and Philadelphia: Falmer Press

Van Daal, V.H.P. and Reitsma, P. (1993) The Use of Speech Feedback by Normal and Disabled Readers in Computer-Based Reading Practice. *Reading and Writing* 5 (3) 243-259.

Vollands, S.R., Topping, K.J. and Evans, H.M. (1996) Experimental Evaluation of Computer-Assisted Self-Assessment of Reading Comprehension: Effects on Reading Achievement and Motivation. Paper delivered at 'Literacy and Technology for the 21st Century' conference, National Reading Research Centre, Atlanta Georgia, October 4-5.

Wangberg, E.G. (1986) An Interactive, Language Experience Based Microcomputer Approach to Reduce Adult Illiteracy. *Lifelong Learning* 9, 8-12.

Wolfendale, S.W. and Topping, K.J. (eds) (1996) *Family Involvement in Literacy: Effective Partnerships in Education.* London and New York: Cassell.

Note

A greatly extended interactive hypertext discussion of electronic literacy by the author will be found in *Reading OnLine*, the electronic journal of International Reading Association.

The author is Director of the Centre for Paired Learning in the Department of Psychology at the University of Dundee, where the effectiveness of methods for non-professionals (such as parents or peers) to tutor others in fundamental skills (eg reading, spelling, writing) and higher order learning (science, maths, etc), across a wide age and ability range and in many different contexts are developed and researched.

For further information: http:\\www.dundee.ac.uk\psychology\c-p-lear.html

13

Literacy: A Shared Responsibility

Sheila Wolfendale

Psychology Department, University of East London

This contribution promotes the view that literacy goals are a collective, societal responsibility and that 'an alliance for literacy' involves all sectors of education, business, industry, community and families. In particular the part that parents/carers and families can play in developing literacy in children and young people is emphasised.

The evolution towards a literate society: an historical perspective

Historical evidence shows us that literate societies such as the Roman and Byzantium Empires, Greece and Egypt have waxed and waned in political power and influence but have bequeathed us wondrous art and literature and their alphabets and orthographies.

Likewise, an historical perspective informs us that literacy concepts and standards have always been relative to particular countries and societies at particular times of their evolution and growth. The following examples show these differing criteria for effective literacy that have pertained at different times in different countries:

- the ability to read religious texts in Sweden in the 17th century

- basic functional literacy, to read and write, characteristic of Britain in the 19th century

- rote learning, mechanical letter and word recognition in France in the 19th century

- reading linked to text comprehension in the USA in the late 19th century. (For sources and further reading see Resnick and Resnick, 1977 and Levine, 1986)

Only in this, the 20th century, have expectations of literacy competency gone beyond these criteria to incorporate 'higher order' literacy functions and we have developed an array of test instruments to assess varying levels of competence.

Before state-provided education, responsibility for teaching reading and literacy was assumed by religious orders, charity schools, small dame schools, philanthropists such as Thomas Coram and Robert Owen – even, clandestinely, by catholics in Ireland during the 17th and 18th centuries, who provided 'hedge schools' (ad hoc, impromptu, secret lessons pro-vided in the countryside) to teach the classics and maintain Gaelic culture.

Gradually the state has assumed responsibility for education and school curricula have become increasingly prescribed and regulated.

Literacy: a common agenda

The concern with literacy is enduring and perennial: society's views and definitions of literacy may change, standards may be perceived to rise or fall (Brooks et al, 1995), but there is always consensus that literacy teach-ing and learning is an educational priority

There is less consensus about the means for achieving these aspirations. At least let us identify and articulate those areas that for example, teachers and parents would agree comprise their literacy goals for children

• reading for pleasure and information

• using the printed word to understand and make sense of the world

• using a range of media

• using language competently in all its rich and varied ways (Wolfendale, 1992).

These shared aspirations have obtained for many years; the particular contemporary 'literacy relativities' that many teachers and parents would want to add to the above list would be:

• the entitlement of bi and multilingual pupils to have opportunities to become fluently literate in their home/community language(s) as well as English (Gregory, 1996)

- the recognition that all pupils need opportunities to become familiar and confident, as much with traditional means of communication, as with the 'new literacies' of information technology and the newer means of communication such as fax, electronic mail, CD Rom, and other forms of multi and interactive media.

Family Literacy: effective partnerships in education?

The burgeoning literature on parental involvement in reading and family literacy provides a body of evidence for the power and effectiveness of 'learning alliances' comprising teachers, parents and pupils initiatives to develop reading achievement.

The early projects explored techniques to maximise 'parents as tutors' such as paired and shared reading (see Topping and Wolfendale, 1985 for a review of the various techniques) and paved the way for broader concepts of family literacy (and see Wolfendale and Topping, 1996 for accounts of this evolution), which can embrace more family members and target the literacy needs of parents too. The recent government-funded Family Literacy Demonstration Projects in four locations provide strong evidence that early family literacy programmes provide

- early introduction to literacy concepts and beginning reading for young pupils

- opportunities for parents (mostly mothers) to 'refresh' and develop their literacy attainment (Brooks et al, 1996).

The advent of fourteen literacy centres in fourteen local education authorities and inclusion by the Department for Education and Employment into current inservice programmes for teachers of grants to support family literacy, ensures continuing opportunities to develop the shared agenda. For it is acknowledged now that parents, irrespective of their own literacy and educational levels, bring so much as 'loving carers' to the 'learning alliance'. Research also demonstrates just how much children's early home experiences do provide formative literacy learning opportunities which teachers need to know about and acknowledge as their starting point for teaching 'schooled literacy' (Weinberger, 1996).

Sharing Responsibility for Literacy – a strategic agenda for education

For educationalists, top of the 'shared agenda' should be the active harnessing of parental interest, commitment and skills to help achieve literacy goals. These suggested strategies are realistic and realisable:

- all schools to have a literacy policy which includes active family literacy programmes

- such programmes will be commensurate with and appropriate to each phase of education, i.e

  - nursery/beginning school: teachers to acknowledge 'home literacy' experiences and work with parents/carers on early literacy concepts and beginning reading

  - early primary (KS1): teachers and parents to: work jointly on early reading and literacy skill areas and literature; promote home-based and schooled literacy learning

  - later primary (KS2): teachers and parents to teach and consolidate 'intermediate' reading and literacy skills and literature in school and home settings

  - iv. secondary (KS3 and 4): teachers and parents to work jointly on higher-order reading and literacy stages, involving advanced reading/comprehension techniques and fostering enjoyment of literature.

At all phases these endeavours to be supported by appropriate use of information technology.

Teachers will be supported by senior staff and will be in receipt of in-service training to achieve these goals; schools will be supported by their LEAs and local literacy centres; OFSTED will include in its national framework for inspection, expectations by which literacy and family literacy 'performance indicators' will be judged.

Such a programme of action over the next few years is achievable without massive financial investment – research has paved the way, the expertise and techniques are available. Let our collective commitment provide the inspiration and impetus for such a concerted effort to raise literacy standards.

References

Brooks, G, Foxman, T, Gorman, T (1995) Standards in Literacy and Numeracy 1948-122 National Commission on Education Briefing, New Series no. 7, NCE, 344-354 Gray's Inn Road, London, WCIX 8BP

Brooks, G, Gorman, T, Harman, J, Hutchison, D, Wilkin, A (1996) Family Literacy Works, the NFER evaluation of the Basic Skills Agency's Demonstration Programmes, BSA, 7th Floor, Commonwealth House, 1-19 New Oxford Street, London, WC1A INU

Gregory, E (1996) Making Sense of a New World: Learning to read in a second language. London. Paul Chapman Publishing

Levine, K (1986) The Social Context of Literacy, London, Routledge

Resnick, D and Resnick, L (1977) The Nature of Literacy, an historical exploration, Harvard Educational Review, Vol. 47, No. 3, August, pp. 370-385

Topping, K and Wolfendale, S (Eds) (1985) Parental Involvement in Children's Reading. London, Croom Helm

Wolfendale, S (1992) Empowering Parents and Teachers – working for Children, London, Cassell

Wolfendale, S and Topping, K (Eds)(1996) Family involvement in Literacy – effective partnerships in education, London, Cassell

14

More Than Just Reading and Writing

David Wray

School of Education, University of Exeter

Although the teaching of literacy and standards of achievement in it have generated considerable controversy and debate over the past decade, there have been surprisingly few attempts to tackle what might be felt to be a fairly fundamental question. Just why is it so important to build a literate nation – in other words, what use is literacy?

At one level, the answer to this is, of course, obvious. People who cannot read and write are cut off from huge swathes of public and community life and have to rely on the input from others to negotiate their ways through a society increasingly dependent upon texts, of one kind or another, as carriers of social discourse. Although it is only recently that technology such as the telephone and the tape recorder appeared to be moving advanced society back towards a more orally based culture, the last few years have seen increased textualisation as electronic communication, via fax, e-mail and the Internet, has reinforced the absolute necessity for dealing with the written word.

At another level, the sheer ubiquity of text has important implications for school learning. Text is the most apparent mediator of learning in virtually all areas of education. We have even adopted the term text-book to describe the most commonly used tool for learning world-wide. There have been many attempts to treat this centrality of text seriously and to provide guidance on ways of maximising the efficiency of pupils learning through text, the best known in this country being perhaps the post-Bullock report Language across the Curriculum movement and the Schools Council projects of the late 70s and early 80s (Lunzer and Gardner, 1979, 1984). Yet, with the best will in the world, these attempts can hardly be said to have succeeded.

There is a clear need for a serious examination of just what learning through text might mean, how it might best be encouraged and developed and what effective teachers of literacy as a means of learning need to know and be able to do. Our own research at the University of Exeter, as part of the Nuffield-funded EXEL (Exeter Extending Literacy) Project, has suggested some interesting lines of inquiry (See Lewis and Wray, 1996 and Wray and Lewis, 1997 for further details). We began with an initial concern to develop teaching strategies which primary teachers might use to help their children use information books in more profitable ways than simple copying out of sections. We have since expanded what we were doing to look at how literacy works, and can be made to work better, as a means of accessing the curriculum. Our current research agenda focuses on secondary school pupils with learning difficulties and on bilingual learners.

What has emerged from the project so far is threefold:

• We have outlined a descriptive model of the process of learning with text. This EXIT (Extending Interactions with Texts) model (Wray and Lewis, 1995) is not intended to be a linear description of stages through which readers go, yet many teachers have found it helpful in terms of offering a guide to the uses of literacy they are trying to teach (Lewis, M., Wray, D. and Mitchell, C., 1995). It draws attention to the need to see learning as an interaction between what is already known and what is new as well as the priority of purpose in reading to learn. A crucial part of the model is its highlighting of the need to develop readers' awareness of their own understanding of text. There is a good deal of research to suggest that this self-awareness can be the crucial factor in the development of effective literacy (Wray, 1994).

• We have developed, and trialled in many classrooms across the country, a variety of teaching strategies which can help teachers develop the literacy of their pupils through a range of curriculum areas. Perhaps the most widely used of these strategies has been our Writing Frames (Lewis and Wray, 1995) which provide pupils with scaffolded support in writing in a variety of genres. The writing which young children have been enabled to produce through careful use of these frames has often staggered us by its quality and effectiveness. Use of the frames has also encouraged many teachers to think seriously about the role and nature of writing in different curriculum areas.

• Finally we have developed a model to describe effective teaching in this area of extending literacy. This model highlights the importance of teachers demonstrating literacy skills to pupils, modelling the ways they tackle particular literacy tasks and giving pupils access, through their talk, to the thinking which underpins these activities. It also recognises the place of collaboration in effective learning. Its major contribution, though, has been to operationalise the concept of scaffolding pupils' learning in literacy. This concept has been a major source of theoretical discussion as we have rediscovered Vygotskian ideas about learning, yet has often seemed very difficult to put into practice in busy classrooms. Many of the teaching strategies we have explored work as scaffolds to pupils' learning and their use gives a practical dimension to an important theoretical concept.

Our work is, of course, only one way of approaching the question of how literacy might best be developed as a means of learning across the school curriculum. It has as a considerable strength that it has developed entirely in collaboration with practising teachers and its theorising is firmly grounded in classroom practice.

It does, of course, raise several further issues to do with teacher education and professional development. We have presented our ideas now to literally thousands of teachers across the country and an interesting reaction we often get is 'Why has nobody ever told us about these things before?' A possible answer to this question is that the issue of using literacy to learn has never really been taken seriously enough by researchers, practitioners and others with educational interests. If we have contributed in a small way to redressing this, that would be an enormous achievement. Literacy is far too important, empowering and enabling for its development to be confined entirely to the early years of schooling.

References

Lewis, M. and Wray, D. (1995) *Developing Children's Non-fiction Writing* Leamington Spa: Scholastic

Lewis, M., Wray, D. and Mitchell, C. (1995) Extending interactions with texts: theory into practice, in *Reading*, Vol 29, No. 1

Lunzer, E. and Gardner, K. (1979) *The Effective Use of Reading* Oxford: Heinemann

Lunzer, E. and Gardner, K. (1984) *Learning from the Written Word* Oxford: Heinemann

Wray, D. (1994) *Literacy and Awareness* Sevenoaks: Hodder and Stoughton

Wray, D. and Lewis, M. (1995) Extending interactions with non-fiction texts: an EXIT into understanding, in *Reading*, Vol 29, No. 1

Wray, D. and Lewis, M. (1997) *Extending Literacy: Reading and Writing Non-fiction in the Primary School* London: Routledge

Part 2

Contributions from organisations in the literacy field

15
Adult Dyslexia Organisation (ADO)

Donald Schloss
Chairman
and Melanie Jameson
Education Adviser

Adult Dyslexia Organisation (ADO) was established in 1991 to advance the cause of adults with dyslexia through research, education, campaigning, lobbying and training. Our services include:

*   a helpline

*   referrals for assessments, tuition and counselling

*   provision of a wide range of information including a regular magazine and a website

*   establishing support groups

*   organising conferences and training.

ADO works to promote the special abilities associated with dyslexia, being a 'dyslexic-run' organisation. Through constant monitoring of enquiries, we are uniquely placed to identify the needs of adult dyslexics and service providers, and re-evaluate our priorities as necessary.

We aim to promote realistic understanding of the implications of dyslexia for adults in the workplace, community organisations, professional bodies/ institutions and throughout the post-16 education sector.

ADO, 336 Brixton Road, London SW9 7AA
Helpline: 0171 924 9559 Admin: 0171 737 7646 Fax: 0171 207 7796
Email: dyslexia.hq@dial.pipex.com
Website: http:www//futurenet.co.uk/charity/ado/index.html (Dyslexia 2000)

The ADO's Agenda for Literacy

Introduction

Despite the efforts of schools and literacy schemes, many adults are still disadvantaged by an inadequate standard of literacy. This is particularly true of the dyslexic community who make up about 4% of the population. This 'hidden handicap' is now recognised as a registered disability in the Chronically Sick and Disabled Persons' Act (1970), the Education Act (1993) and the Disability Discrimination Act (1995).

The Adult Dyslexia Organisation asserts that adults with dyslexia do not necessarily benefit from standard Adult Literacy provision due to the nature of dyslexic difficulties and the compensating strategies employed.

Dyslexic difficulties in relation to literacy

Although dyslexia is commonly perceived as a spelling/reading problem, it is better described as a chronic difficulty in processing certain sorts of information, linked to a weak short-term memory. Since reading may not be automatic and skimming effectively through text is seldom possible, the majority of dyslexics remain word-by-word readers. Reading skills may be further compromised by visual perceptual problems when print appears to shift, or 'glare' from white paper obscures the text.

Writing speed may be slow and copying laborious. Where handwriting is poor, practice may not lead to any improvement.

Dyslexia is increasingly regarded as a 'difference in learning style' – this is particularly true with spelling, explaining the minimal progress often made in conventional literacy classes and supporting the argument for specially trained tutors. Tuition must both draw on the strengths associated with dyslexia (such as powers of visualisation, the ability to formulate an overview) and accommodate the weaknesses.

Many dyslexic adults in employment are obliged to turn down promotion because of anticipated increased demands on reading and writing skills and remain in unfulfilling basic level employment. In other cases, poor literacy skills form a barrier to gaining employment.

Most dyslexic adults live with the anxiety that their literacy problems will be exposed; however the decision to tackle literacy problems is never taken lightly. The humiliation suffered at school inevitably makes them unwilling to 'risk education' again. It is therefore vital that they encounter informed understanding and appropriate expertise to avoid reinforcing feelings of failure and inadequacy.

As an organisation, ADO is particularly aware of the needs of those who are disadvantaged by other factors in addition to the burden of dyslexia. Members of ethnic minorities can be disadvantaged because dyslexic difficulties are often attributed to cultural factors and the fact that English may not be the first language.

Our agenda for literacy

ADO proposes a multiple response to the complex issues involved in improving access to and provision of suitable literacy schemes. A three pronged approach is essential to tackle the problem of underachievement amongst dyslexic adults:

- increasing targeted publicity promoting understanding of dyslexia in adults

- the promotion of appropriate screening and tutor training programmes

- the employment of a trained dyslexia tutor on every adult literacy scheme.

Publicity should be targeted at the workplace, the Employment Service, community centres and literacy schemes; the special features of each will be considered below.

a) The workplace

An ADO study (1994) revealed that 89% of employers sampled felt they had no dyslexic employees. ADO therefore intends to expand its activities in the workplace, contacting more companies and informing personnel departments of the needs of dyslexic employees. This is particularly important where staff development programmes form part of promotion procedures.

ADO encourages the provision of workplace literacy schemes, stressing that these must take the special features of dyslexia into account. (Our Education Adviser can provide details of methodology and tuition materials.)

We currently produce comprehensive information packs for employers, employees and the unemployed; these are now being revised, in conjunction with the DFEE, to cover the Disability Discrimination Act. Inherent weaknesses within the new act may cause dyslexic employees, threatened with dismissal because of their disability, to turn to their Unions. We therefore foresee closer links with Trade Unions (as have been achieved with the CPSA) to enable them to disseminate information and provide support.

b) The Employment Service

It is important that the services available to dyslexic people be clearly displayed in all Job Centres for the benefit of staff and clients. Dyslexic adults should be referred to the Disability Employment Advisor (DEA) and assessed by an Occupational Psychologist if necessary. If 'rehabilitation' is advised, this should be provided by trained dyslexia specialists, since standard literacy provision is less likely to benefit dyslexic people. It is therefore necessary for each area team to have a contract with a dyslexia specialist who can deliver programmes based on the specific needs of their clients, taking literacy and vocational factors into account.

c) Community centres and ethnic minorities

Cultural differences and the use of languages other than English are sometimes given as a reason for low achievement, completely over-looking the factor of dyslexia. Our current publicity demonstrates our multi-racial outlook and underlines our commitment to serving all our members. ADO is committed to the training of community-based tutors from ethnic minorities so that dyslexia is catered for in community literacy schemes (such as those run by housing organisations).

ADO recently piloted a project in Brixton to reach dyslexics from ethnic minorities and inform them how to access help/support. We believe there is much need for the expansion of such projects.

d) Literacy centres

Literacy programmes are a key stepping stone for adults wishing to return to education; it is therefore regrettable that several major bodies in the field do not currently have a policy on dyslexia. Unfortunately many dyslexic adults drop out of classes and abandon the attempt to tackle their literacy problems because they have not received appropriate tuition and understanding. Dyslexic adults may need the support of trained counsellors to help them overcome the trauma they associate with education.

Although staff inset days may include dyslexia awareness, these are not compulsory; many tutors are therefore not trained to identify dyslexia. ADO maintains that each centre should have at least one tutor trained to teach dyslexic adults and that all tutors should be able to administer a screening test to all new students.

ADO is surveying current provision to identify the following:

* gaps in provision
* willingness of tutors to adapt to the needs of adult dyslexics
* the level of expertise currently available.

Priorities for funding

ADO's funding priorities reflect our Agenda for Literacy. However, targeted publicity and awareness raising will not be effective unless those who come forward with literacy difficulties can be directed towards suitable help which, in turn, is dependent on the availability of trained tutors.

Tutor training

Since literacy tuition is delivered in a wide range of circumstances there are many variables to consider. Within colleges/literacy centres, volunteer tutors are often used to provide 1:1 support. In the workplace, training may be delivered by an agency. Careers officers and community organisations have their specific networks.

ADO believes that the following general principles should apply: tutors should be trained in presenting a highly structured programme combining 'overlearning', visualisation techniques and a multisensory approach whereby spelling is taught using different senses as reinforcement. Sensitivity to the vulnerability of dyslexic students is essential for tutor and volunteer. A careful balance must be struck between sympathetic and informed understanding and a patronising approach.

ADO will continue to support tutors in the following ways:

* compiling details of suitable training courses for literacy tutors

* providing guidance on the administration of a screening test or checklist

* recommending teaching materials and updating reference materials

* listing appropriate reading schemes for adult dyslexics with literacy difficulties

* encouraging the employment of one dyslexia specialist on all literacy schemes.

Two final components are necessary:

* the voices of dyslexics themselves must be heard through the contributions of user led groups and

* there must be full student involvement in learning.

16
The Arts Council of England

Dr. Alastair Niven

Director of Literature

The Arts Council of England is a successor body to the Arts Council of Great Britain (ACGB) which was established in 1946. On 1 April 1994, the ACGB's responsibilities and functions were transferred to three new bodies: the Arts Council of England, the Scottish Arts Council and the Arts Council of Wales. The Arts of Council of Northern Ireland was already established as a separate body.

The Arts Council of England is the main funding agency for the arts in England. It is a publicly accountable body which distributes public money to a wide range of arts organisations and projects. It operates under a Royal Charter granted in 1994 in which its objectives are stated as:

* to develop and improve the knowledge, understanding and practice of the arts

* to increase the accessibility of the arts to the public

* to advise and co-operate with departments of government, local authorities, the Arts Councils for Scotland, Wales and Northern Ireland and other bodies.

Address: The Arts Council of England, 14 Great Peter Street, LONDON SW1 3NQ.

Telephone: 0171 333 0100 Fax: 0171 973 6590

The Arts Council of England and Literacy

The Arts Council of England's Royal Charter is dedicated to the creation of new art and to widening access to and understanding of it. Officially, therefore, we have no view of literacy issues. These, we could maintain with a poker face, are best left to those whose training and skills make them expert in a particularly sensitive field.

In fact the work of the Literature department of the Arts Council predicates an ability to read. Most of the writing we fund is contemporary – not so banal a point as it may sound because other art departments at the Council spend considerable sums on subsidising classical repertoires in dance, drama and music. All funding decisions, at least within the Treasury grant (lottery funding is experimenting with new approaches), are taken on the basis of artistic merit. Put the two factors together – new work assessed qualitatively – and you have a body of writing, published in books and journals, which is by its nature challenging and often at the cutting edge of new forms and topics. It would be hypocritical to pretend that such work is an easy read or could be assimilated by people with poor literacy skills.

How then does the Arts Council Literature policy fulfil the needs of less educated people or those with impaired faculties? It is a difficult question and sometimes one feels that it is politically incorrect even to raise it because it may have a patronising aspect to it. In addition we are from time to time reminded by the press that we are not a social service or an agency for therapeutic counselling. This is a knee-jerk reaction to schemes which could be interpreted as socially interventionist: placing writers in prisons and hospices, for example, or funding specialist literary journals for black people, or assisting students at Open University summer schools to enjoy personal contact with writers.

Our task is twofold. On the one hand we do everything we can within our budgetary constraints to help good new writing to come into existence. We also, however, regard the widening of readerships as paramount. Indeed, it is difficult to have a strategy to create brilliant new writing, much though one may encourage the context in which it can happen. No five-year arts plan can decree that in a particular year there will be another *Middlemarch* or new collection of poems comparable in their revolutionary effect to Wordsworth's *Lyrical Ballads* or T.S. Eliot's *The Wasteland*. If, however, great writing cannot be made to order even in the most comprehensive arts strategy, great reading can be. The Arts Councils (and I feel confident in evoking the Arts Councils of Scotland, Northern Ireland and Wales in this, alongside that of England) can systematically identify groups of people where the intervention of public money from the arts sector may make a difference.

At the Arts Council of England, for instance, we prioritise disabled people in every area of our work, not just in literature. No one is written out of the script because they cannot walk, see, hear, or respond. There are special programmes to ensure that women, black and Asian people, homosexuals, rural dwellers and the young are given equal opportunities to practice and enjoy the arts. All these are easy targets for ill-disposed critics of the Arts Council, but they rarely come up with arguments that go beyond the airing of prejudice.

The Literature department emphasises the importance of getting young people to read – one reason why we so welcome the National Reading Initiative which Joanna Trollope is chairing. We run a biennial Children's Literature Summer School in Oxford which brings together teachers, librarians and booksellers engaged with young people's reading. We support as many initiatives as we can which will widen opportunities for the young to encounter books, of almost any kind. We would rather that people read something than nothing. And the process can begin at the beginning and go on until the end. Books for babies and assistance to the retired and housebound are of equal value.

All this may seem a long way from literacy. We repeat, we have no specific brief or expertise in literacy matters. We passionately believe, however, that the literary experience can and must touch everyone. This becomes increasingly apparent as we approach a new century where advances in medicine and changes in social and economic conditions will inevitably create millions more people with reading time at their disposal. Reading is one of the greatest delights in life, the masterly route to imagination and knowledge. Literacy is its keystone. The Arts Council, *quod erat demonstrandum*, lends its backing to all those who seek to encourage wider literacy. Our role as funders will continue to be the support of new writing and readerships, which are the fruits of literacy, but our advocacy will be as much for the central cause of literacy itself.

17

The Basic Skills Agency

Jim Pateman

Senior Development Officer

The Basic Skills Agency (BSA) is the national agency for literacy, numeracy and related basic skills for England and Wales. Although funded primarily by central government it is an independent organisation with a Board of Management that includes representatives of local education authorities, Training and Enterprise Councils, employers, trade unions, voluntary organisations, further education colleges and other national and training organisations.

The BSA is committed to improving standards of basic skills and works with others, including schools, colleges, local education authorities, industry and the national and local organisations involved in education and training.

It provides a wide range of organisations with advice and support to develop high quality programmes to help children, young people and adults to improve their basic skills.

Address: The Basic Skills Agency, Commonwealth House, 1-19 New Oxford Street, London, WC1A 1NU. Telephone: 0171 405 4017 Fax: 0171 440 6626

The Strategic Agenda for Tackling Basic Skills Difficulties

Over the past five years the issue of literacy and the debate on standards of literacy, both in and after school, has moved up the public agenda. The preoccupation has moved from 'is there a problem?' to 'what do we as a country do about it?' The Basic Skills Agency has been involved in many of the developments to tackle the problems of young people and adults; and we are now working to support initiatives with children in primary and secondary education. We are taking stock of our activities, and how we might operate in the next three years and beyond.

It now seems widely accepted that we have a major problem with under-education in the UK. Higher education compares well with most industrialised countries and we produce as many well-qualified people at graduate level as the United States, France and Germany. We compare poorly, however, at a lower level, and too many young people leave school without any formal qualifications. This represents a waste of potential that we cannot afford. The effect in terms of skills shortages, loss of competitiveness and cost to industry have been demonstrated through a number of research programmes.

Most other industrialised countries have a similar problem to ours, including the USA, Canada, Australia, and our EU partners. The recent White Paper on competitiveness is not very conclusive about whether we're better or worse. It's claimed that Pacific Rim countries don't have a basic skills problem but this may be because of very low thresholds and definitions. International surveys will form part of the debate over the coming five years. It is to be hoped, however, that they provide a spur to action, rather than a series of sterile blame-sessions.

And what of the cost to the individual? Well, it's important to retain a perspective. There are far more serious disadvantages than having poor basic skills. It is not the educational equivalent of AIDs. Many adults with poor basic skills are happy with their lives, are fulfilled and contribute.

But let's not pretend that it doesn't matter. Let's not continue to insult those with poor basic skills with the argument that all skills are equal – the '*I can't change a plug, you can't read and write*' nonsense. Most of these adults (and children with difficulties) know the degree of pretence being exercised here. They should not be the guinea pigs for someone else's ideological engineering.

Our research has consistently shown the handicap that adults with poor literacy skills suffer. They are likely to be unemployed more often, and for longer[1]. The increasing demand for adequate basic skills among employers means that fewer and fewer jobs will be open to them[2]. There are clear links between poor basic skills and levels of homelessness and crime[3].

The graphs on page 96 illustrate the effect of low levels of basic skills on young men and women. The problems that they face in finding and getting work and the 'exclusion' that they face from other aspects of adult life, are stark and urgent.

So, it's an important issue that must be dealt with, on both an individual and societal level. It's important to the health of the nation, today as much as in the nineteenth century, when the expansion of literacy and the extension of democracy were interlinked.

What measures must we take as a nation to start the process of tackling basic skills difficulties? Although a variety of measures are already in place to try to prevent failure, to raise standards in schools and help adults to improve essential basic skills, more needs to be done. An increase in the level of competence required, population growth and movement, and the current level of take-up of basic skills programmes could make our problem worse in the next century, rather than better.

In simple terms any strategy needs to:

• **ensure that initial and preventive measures work effectively enough so that fewer and fewer children 'seep' through and require additional help in school or after school**

• **take measures to allow children, young people and adults to 'catch up' or improve their shaky basic skills.**

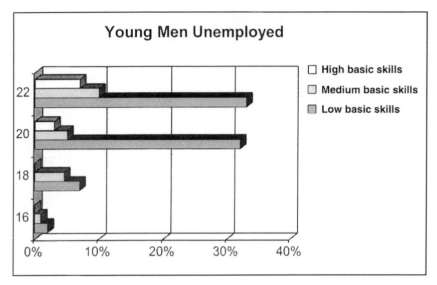

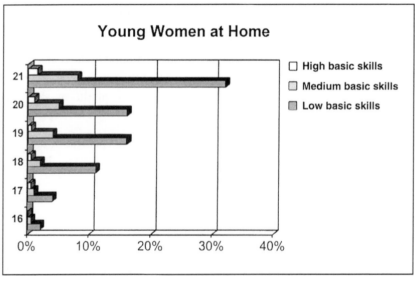

Prevention

Action to make sure that this 'seepage' is reduced should include:

- a review of the ways in which the implementation of the National Curriculum assists or hinders the development of good literacy skills

- regular assessment of literacy levels and progress throughout compulsory schooling

- the expansion of nursery provision, with an emphasis on achieving 'reading-readiness'

- the reform of initial teacher training, so that teachers at both primary and secondary levels are better equipped to teach reading, writing and spelling

- family literacy programmes, that do much to reduce the disadvantages that children face when they start school, as well as improving the involvement and skills of their parents[4].

Catch-up

Action here should include:

- many of the current school-based programmes such as Reading Recovery

- intensive, motivating programmes at Key Stage 4

- improved in-service training

- school/industry link programmes

- training programmes for the unemployed, including Youth Training and programmes for adults. These must provide prioritised opportunities for those with basic skills problems, rather than exclude them just because they require more support and are more 'expensive' to train

- 'primary' basic skills programmes run by colleges and LEAs

- basic skills support in colleges

- workplace-based programmes that represent a bargain between employers and employees to improve basic skills that enhance employability and effectiveness at work

- government programmes that harness the commitment and enthusiasm of individuals, communities, employers, local authorities and others in regeneration projects. For many, improvements in literacy will provide a 'gateway' into many of these programmes.

Initial and preventive measures are of paramount importance because additional help is expensive in financial terms and for the individual in personal terms. Many people in basic skills programmes at say age 35 have cost a good deal in terms of additional help in school and post-school. Poor basic skills have also probably cost them much stigma, self-esteem and lost opportunities. In personal terms their employment has suffered and they have not been able to contribute to the development of a flexible well-trained workforce. The intergenerational impact is well known. Family Literacy programmes have demonstrated the strong motivation that many parents with poor basic skills have to help their children avoid the problems they have encountered. However, it will always be more difficult and costly to tackle the problems of adults, than to try to intervene during the compulsory phases of education.

Nevertheless, 'catch up' measures are important because of the 'backlog'. Even if initial teaching becomes much more effective we have to provide opportunities for all of those – children, young people and adults – for whom effectiveness from now on is too late. This will be costly but if the strategy works, costs should go down as 'seepage' gets less and more benefit from catch up measures.

And we must learn to target better. Many of the children and adults that need help are not far behind. We have had to counteract the notion, much trumpeted in some of the press, that there are 6,000,000 'illiterates' in the adult population. Similarly, the end of Key Stage assessment data, shown on page 99, throughout the Key Stages, shows that the largest group under-attaining are just one level behind.

Any strategy that attempts a blanket approach, a single quick fix, is certain to fail. But programmes that include a clear focus on those

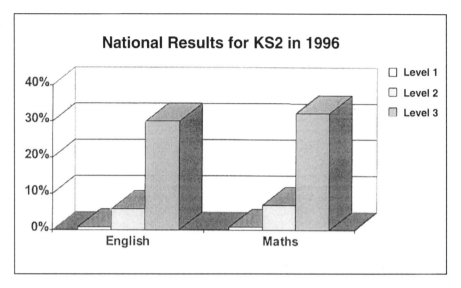

children and adults with some, but inadequate skills, will provide a better chance of moving large numbers of the basic skills 'have nots' into the 'haves'. The benefits? Greater numbers of young people and adults will be able to respond to the challenges that they face as individuals, and that the nation faces as a whole. Many organisations, agencies and individuals will need to be mobilised to ensure a high-level, not half-hearted response. And there will be a need for Government, national and local to take a lead in supporting and co-ordinating what must be a National Campaign, that lasts a number of years and produces a series of lasting gains.

References

1   Literacy, Numeracy and Adults, *Basic Skills Agency*

2   Basic Skills and Jobs, *Basic Skills Agency*

3   Literacy, Numeracy and Adults, *Basic Skills Agency*; Basic Skills and Prisons, *Basic Skills Agency*

4   Family Literacy Works, *Basic Skills Agency*

18
British Dyslexia Association

Paul Cann

Director

The BDA represents all children and adults with specific learning difficulties, a population estimated at some two million people in this country alone. We campaign for change to improve the opportunities available for dyslexic people, but we do so with our feet on the ground of a grassroots member-ship of some 8,000 members in affiliated local associations, 60 corporate member organisations and 1000 members of the mailing-list.

We run Helplines, a Befriender service, Computer Co-ordinators, a wide range of publications, a membership development programme, and other services. Our most strategic function is to lobby and campaign for the longer-term changes. This will continue in the future, extending our current campaign for better teacher training and early intervention, and developing it to include a range of work on behalf of dyslexic adults.

Address: British Dyslexia Association, 98 London Road, READING RG1 5AU.

Admin: 01189 662677 Helpline: 01189 66871 Fax: 01189 351 927

Climbing the Mountain Together

We need literacy to communicate, and without communication we can not in any positive sense survive. Our agenda should therefore target the communication skills needed, both for success at the national level of the economy, and also fulfilment of potential at the level of the individual. Four themes will run throughout this quest:

- achieving **general ownership** of the challenge: literacy is the responsibility of all of us, and it is time that all sectors of the community recognised their own rightful obligations and those of other parties

- bringing the players together in **partnership**, so that all available resources are harnessed and used to their fullest extent

- dissecting the **challenge into its component parts**, understanding those different parts, and setting targets for progress which are sensible given the nature of those component challenges

- equipping our schools with the **expertise** required to answer the multi-faceted challenge of literacy.

Ownership of the challenge

We must come together and agree that we have a joint stake in this. Literacy is not to be passed off as the job of parents or teachers; it is the job of all of us, each agency or constituency with its different responsibilities. Any other approach leads to the culture of recriminatory glares over the shoulder, rather than looking ahead in joint problem-solving. Obvious, yet we waste a great deal of time on recrimination

Projects such as the Literacy Collaborative, initiated by the National Literacy Trust in Newcastle, or the Reading is Fundamental projects, seek to secure just such a joint ownership. The intention is to reaffirm that the whole city cares about literacy, and commits itself to a long-term programme of work to make progress. Work for literacy becomes a badge of honour or a flame held aloft, and is thus elevated above it being seen too narrowly as a priority for educationalists.

But what is surprising about these initiatives is that there are so few of them. If literacy is so dear to us, as politicians from all sides appear to agree, why hasn't every city in the land adopted this approach. Why do we collectively not value and celebrate this crucial communication skill? Why do more communities not see that these basic skills are the means to break out of the prison of poverty and disadvantage and place literacy at the very top of the common agenda?

A key aim of the strategic agenda for literacy should be to ensure that in every part of the country there is a collective renewal of commitment to this as the burning issue – a master-key which will unlock many doors in addition to the room marked, say, 'National Curriculum'.

Using the available resources in partnership

Having taken the important step of establishing a 'community commit-ment' to literacy, there is hard work to be done in ensuring that the con-siderable resources already in play are used to better effect. Higher value for literacy will inevitably mean some re-ordering of commitments in favour of literacy. But we need at the same time to be aware that there will never be enough resources, and the issue then becomes to be clear about what we do have and how we might use what we do have more effectively.

In our work with schools for children with special educational needs we repeatedly witness the difficulties schools face in identifying and harnessing resources to help such vulnerable children. The problems are varied. At a basic level it is often a question of knowing what resources are available through the funding formula to support children at the less severe, pre-formal statementing stages. It is shocking how little is known by people in schools who ought to know – such as members of governing bodies – about the true level of resources available.

Beyond the basic facts of identifying duties and resources, it is also a question of team work to solve literacy problems. So often the people concerned with supporting children with literacy difficulties do not work properly together – the school governor doesn't champion the Special Educational Needs Co-ordinator, the class teacher doesn't inform and involve the parents as they would wish, the specialist teacher operates in a vacuum, and so on... Effective partnerships can make all the difference between a fragmented and incoherent approach to support for children who find it hard to read or write. Yet, as publicly funded reports and our own experience show, they do not happen often enough.

As a national voluntary organisation representing the many children and adults with specific literacy difficulties, we are dismayed at how often our potential contribution goes to waste because a national agency or public body fails to consult or involve us and tap into the energy and expertise our members would willingly provide. This is not a matter of organisational ego-building but rather a statement that all who have something to offer must be included. The literacy challenge needs a wide ownership and partnership.

These are simple examples of the way we waste resources that are there already. Without spending a single extra pound of public money we could transform the quality of literacy support in our schools. The strategic agenda for literacy must include a progression beyond sloganising – 'partnership with parents', 'whole school policies' and their like – so that the principle of collective ownership of the literacy challenge finds a reality in day-to-day partnerships.

Versatile expertise for a multifaceted challenge

Literacy is a broad term, concealing a rich variety of challenges. It is crucial that we analyse the subject carefully, and understand that there are many different components which need to be discussed. Applying any kind of broad brush – for example by advocating a particular methodology and by implication rubbishing others – will not do. We must be looking for the different ways in which children acquire language and literacy skills, and the many different obstacles to that process which may materialise.

Dyslexia is an example of a component part which needs to be understood separately from other obstacles to literacy, such as social deprivation (though often the two are inter-related). We now know that dyslexia has biological origins, to which there is a genetic dimension, and that its effects result from differences in the brain which make language-processing more problematic. The challenge is to understand these effects, and indeed that dyslexia itself is a multi-faceted term. To tackle this component of the problem we need particular tools and techniques, and those involved in literacy teaching need to understand this.

As we discover more and more about the human brain, its intricacies and individuality, we learn more about understanding and responding to those differences in literacy teaching.. The final element in the strategic agenda must be about the skills required to teach literacy – which includes skills of learning and thinking – successfully.

Thus the strategy must include a radical review of the training and professional development we give to our teachers, with our sights set on the long term of a more versatile and skilled profession. When a recently completed survey by the University of East London tells us that 3 out of 4 serving teachers feel ill-equipped to cope with dyslexia by their initial teacher training, and to only a slightly lesser extent by their in-service development, and when this survey merely echoes several others calling attention to this shortcoming, alarm bells should be ringing at the Teacher Training Agency, in the Department for Education and Employment and along other corridors of power.

The good news is that we can see some shining examples of literacy initiatives which demonstrate that this is one mountain that can indeed be climbed. But only if we resolve to climb it together.

19

The British Film Institute

Cary Bazalgette

Principal Education Officer

The BFI was founded in 1933 and receives an annual grant from the Department of National Heritage to foster the development of film, television and video in the UK and to enhance public access to and appreciation of these media.

Since 1950 the BFI has campaigned for media teaching to be included in the school curriculum and in further, higher and continuing education. We have done this through conferences, teacher training courses, the support of local and regional initiatives, the development and publication of teaching resources and guides, and through commissioning and publishing research. In the future we plan a greater emphasis on externally-funded research and development, in partnership with other institutions.

Address: The British Film Institute, 21 Stephen Street, London WIP 2LN. Telephone: 0171 255 1444 Fax: 0171 436 7950

Literacy and the Moving Image

Any public debate that couples literacy with the moving image media of film, television and video rarely amounts to more than a dismal litany of declining standards and ill-informed speculation about media 'effects'. Discussion of children's audio-visual experiences always concentrates upon what they should not see and what they should be protected from, than upon what they should see. After one hundred years of moving image culture, it is about time that we faced up to the responsibility of defining what it is that we want children to know about that important heritage, and how we can best encourage them to imagine the creative possibilities of the moving image. This will not be a simple task, to be achieved by making simplistic and short-term demands upon educators. A long-term timescale for change must be acknowledged.

So far, education systems have signally failed to recognise, define, foster and broaden the audio-visual 'literacy' that children already have, based on extensive television and video viewing in the home. Children learn about media from the media, such as cinema, television, video, books, and merchandising, as well as from their peer groups. In all these learning environments, parents play a key role in making purchasing and regulatory choices for their children. But it is now widely acknowledged that schools have a responsibility to take children beyond this informal learning and to develop a more systematic understanding of the moving image media. It is recognised that this is a necessary part of learning about our culture, our society and our democratic processes.

Many countries in Europe now have formal requirements for media education in their national curricula. In some countries young people can opt for specialist courses in media studies at secondary school level. Numerous initiatives and projects over the past 30 years have helped to develop ideas about the forms and methods that media education can take.

In England and Wales, for example, the national curriculum requires that the 'pupils should be introduced to a wide range of media. e.g. magazines, newspapers, radio, television, film. They should be given opportunities to analyse and evaluate such material, which should be of high quality and represent a range of forms and purposes, and different structural and presentational devices' (English, Key Stages 3 and 4, Reading). In Britain some 35,000 young people each year complete examination courses in media studies and related subjects at GCSE, A Level, BTEC, SCOTVEC and GNVQ. The existence of such courses and the specialists who teach them help to spread the idea of studying the media as a valid and interesting activity, not necessarily as a passport to the uncertain world of employment in the media industries, but as a good humanities subject that offers an understanding of society and culture.

However, in general 5-16 schooling there is little consensus about the goals and methods of media education. In addition, there is little initial or in-service training to support it. The inevitable result is that media education provision is patchy, often of low quality, and under-resourced. Where it is of high quality, there are few effective ways of identifying and maintaining high standards and of sharing good practice. In 14-19 education, the expansion of media studies courses has coincided with high staff turnover and diminished INSET provision, resulting in a serious and increasing shortage of qualified media teachers.

• There is therefore an immediate crisis in the teaching and resourcing of media teaching at all levels, despite the growing consensus at policy level that children ought to learn something about the media during their formal education. This crisis needs to be resolved now, with priority given to improving initial and in-service training and to the development of better curriculum guidelines. This is the first agenda item in a strategy for literacy and the moving image.

However, a much larger crisis is waiting just around the corner. More highly compressed software, hugely enhanced computer capacity and broadband networks will very soon allow large numbers of people much fuller access to moving image material than they have ever had before. They will also provide more people with the tools to create, modify and relay moving images themselves. We should beware of underestimating the enormous implications of these developments for the status of print texts. Print will not die, but its place in our culture will change. Indeed, the nature of text will change: new kinds of text are likely to emerge, which combine print with still and moving images, and with sound. How will this affect what children should be learning in school?

The vast overload of information on the new systems due to inappropriate use and excessive expectations will not only lead to a proliferation of policing and mediating services but will also place a premium on critical, evaluative and analytical skills, and knowledge about the sources and regulation of texts in all media.

The competition for attention and status amongst a multiplicity of broadcast and cable channels, and innumerable network sites, will place a premium on creative, communicative and presentational skills in moving image, sound and graphics, often equally with verbal language.

The proliferation of choices and claims for attention from the new forms of media will place a premium on depth and breadth of cultural knowledge, including its historical dimensions.

Applied to media other than print, these are for most people new kinds of skill, knowledge and understanding. Taken together, they could amount to a new definition of what it may mean to be 'literate' in a digital age. Claims for new types of literacy would mean a substantial national commitment over the next five years to research and development that would define the ways in which literacy education needs to change. The agenda items for funding and policy development are as follows:

- the prioritisation of research and development projects that have at least the potential for an extended time-scale, as opposed to short-term projects, however high-profile, in order to favour the development of more reliable models for continuous learning

- the prioritisation of research into how learners best acquire critical and creative skills in relation to moving image media, and the development of resources that best support the development of such skills

- a commitment to extending the notions of 'fair dealing' and 'public domain' in the educational field, so that teachers and learners may have free access to a wider range of texts for purposes of criticism and analysis, and a better appreciation of their media heritage, both national and global.

20

Centre for Language in Primary Education

Dr Myra Barrs

Director

The Centre for Language in Primary Education is a professional development centre based in the London Borough of Southwark specialising in all aspects of primary English. As well as being a resource and consultancy centre for teachers, it produces a wide range of publications. These include:

'The Primary Language Record Handbook' (1988)

'The Reading Book' (1991) – a teacher's guide to reading

'Read it Together' (1995) – a pamphlet for parents

'The Core Book' (1996) – a structured approach to using books in the reading curriculum

Address: Centre for Language in Primary Education, Webber Street, London SE1 8QW

Telephone: 0171 633 0840/ 0171 401 3382/3 Fax: 0171 928 4624
email: clpe@rmplc.co.uk

The Teaching of Literacy in Primary Schools

Today more is expected of education than ever before. Increasing demands are made on the literacy of workers in most fields. This is a relatively new phenomenon. Immediately after the second world war, it was not expected that the majority of the population would need more than a basic education in literacy, indeed the '11 plus' examination was actually designed to fail most pupils. Today, a high standard of education and of literacy for all pupils is regarded as a desirable and achievable goal.

But there is also controversy about *how* to achieve this. The introduction of the national curriculum for English was not treated, as it should have been, as an opportunity to arrive at a consensus agenda for literacy at the end of this century, but instead has been an area of intense ideological infighting. News media have consistently presented schools in general as failing and children as underachieving. The crisis of confidence in schools is not – as it is presented as being – universal. Martin Hughes' research[1] has helpfully shown that most parents are satisfied with their children's primary schooling. However, the repeated media message that things are not well in literacy teaching has been corrosive. It has badly affected morale among teachers, and made it harder to communicate to a wider audience what is actually going on in primary schools. This publication from the National Literacy Trust is helpful, in making a discussion of literacy in education available to a wider audience.

Positive developments

Despite the picture painted above, there have been major positive developments in the teaching of literacy in primary schools in the past twenty years. There is now a much more general understanding of the complexity of the reading process and of the different levels of information that readers need. This understanding has led to changes in practice. More is expected now of children learning to read and write and a more long-term view is taken of literacy development.

We know that, from the outset, readers use all the information they can in order to read, not only their knowledge of letter-sound relationships, but also their awareness of syntax, their familiarity with book language and story, and – not least – their sense of the meaning of the text. Many schools now teach children to draw on *all* these sources of information as they learn to read. The aim is that children should learn to read with understanding and appreciate the satisfactions of reading (children are unlikely to develop as readers if they do not like reading). In the same way, children are now no longer expected to learn to write mainly by copying, but are expected to use writing for communicative purposes from the beginning.

We now think it important that the teaching of reading and writing should continue throughout the primary school, and that children should broaden the range of their reading and writing and be able to use their literacy critically. All of these expectations were reflected in both the first and the second versions of the national curriculum for English.

When schools communicate these high expectations to children, and provide them with the teaching and support they need to develop their literacy fully, standards are high. However, in any education system the challenge is always to ensure that such high standards are general. There will continue to be a need for measures to promote and disseminate effective practices and pedagogical approaches, and for well-targeted investment. Our strategic agenda for literacy for the next five years suggests nine priority areas where future effort and investment could helpfully be directed:

- home and school
- budgeting in the primary sector
- books and resources
- help for children with difficulties
- professional development
- teacher assessment
- research in literacy
- public information
- new literacies.

1. Home and school

In recent years, schools have begun to build more consciously on children's home literacy experiences; parents' parts in teaching their children to read have been acknowledged and supported. Among innovations that might further these developments are:

* statutory time for parents and teachers to meet and discuss children's learning – our experience of these 'parent conferences' (from the Primary Language Record) suggests that they can transform home/school relationships, and influence teaching
* holiday clubs for parents and children, with a literacy focus
* more widely available parent information about books and literacy (eg advice leaflets in health centres, libraries, etc. in all major heritage languages); parent advice services, a TV or video series on literacy.

2. Budgeting in the primary sector

Perhaps the biggest single change that could affect standards of literacy would be the introduction of smaller classes in primary schools, brought about by an equalisation of spending across the primary and secondary sectors. Both primary and secondary schools have the task of teaching the national curriculum, but the resources made available to primary schools have always been lower. This historical accident should end; a bigger investment should be made in the all-important early years of schooling. There should also be a return to previous standards of supplementary funding for areas of greatest need, and for the education of bilingual children.

3. Books and resources

There is unevenness of book provision in schools, which has not been sufficiently highlighted. There should be more measures to ensure improvements:

* National standards of book provision, and national school library standards should be established and included in inspections. These national standards should be included in briefing papers for all involved in the management of schools.

4. Children with difficulties

We have learnt more about how to identify and support reading difficulties. However, more needs to be done to analyse the factors involved in failure, and to disseminate really successful practice. Attention should be focused on:

- the social and gender issues involved in reading failure
- the early identification of children with literacy difficulties, based on record-keeping in normal classroom contexts
- analysis of effective mainstream ways of supporting children with difficulties.

5. Professional development

There will continue to be a need for educational investment to enhance quality of teaching. A recent report on schools which have done badly in OFSTED inspections shows that teachers in such schools often suffer from being professionally isolated.

- Teachers should be encouraged to develop their skills as professionals, with incentives to encourage this (eg increments for further training, further professional qualifications, sabbatical terms for teachers pursuing projects in literacy)
- The number of school-based professional development days (an important innovation) should be doubled, with a certain number each year devoted to literacy.

6. Teacher assessment

Teacher assessment (TA) has never been given real weight in the National Curriculum assessment process, though it has frequently been said to be as important as external assessment (SATs). TA can inform teaching decisions, and provide fuller information for parents than SATs scores do, but more work is needed to support the reliability of TA. This would have an important function in establishing shared standards across schools. Elements that need to be in place are:

- national models of record-keeping (there are still none, despite lip service paid to the importance of teachers' records) and real exemplars from classrooms. The Primary Language Record provides a developed model for this[2,3]
- local and regional moderation meetings where teachers' assessments are shared and moderated.

7. Research in literacy

Despite recent discussions of 'evidence-based teaching', there is a dearth of nationally funded research in education. Moreover, current funding mechanisms do not provide as many opportunities for teacher research as used to be available. We need more research in key areas such as:

- gender and literacy
- developing the uses of literacy for effective learning in all subjects A national archive of children's work and teachers' records would provide a fuller picture of children's long-term literacy development.

8. Public information

Public understanding of literacy teaching and standards of literacy is at the mercy of media. Better information needs to be made more widely available, via:

- newsletters for parents from LEAs
- regular access radio and TV slots for schools
- an in-depth video series about literacy in schools.

9. New literacies

We sometimes see new literacies as competing with traditional literacies, yet there is strong evidence that TV actually promotes reading. Many new literacies (eg the Internet) involve a mass of reading and writing. Possible areas of exploration would be:

- a study of the multimedia experience of young children (eg a longitudinal study could follow young children's literacy development into the 21st century)
- more guidance to parents about new media and discussing them with children.

References

1. Hughes, M. et al (1994) *Parents and their Children's Schools* Oxford: Blackwell

2. Barrs, M, S. Ellis, H. Hester and A. Thomas (1988) *The Primary Language Record Handbook* London, CLPE

3. *Using the Primary Language Record Reading Scales* (1996) London, CLPE

21
The Dyslexia Institute

Liz Brooks

Executive Director

The Dyslexia Institute was established in 1972 as an educational charity to provide:
* assessment
* teaching
* teacher-training
* advice and information.

In 1996 our 375 teachers, support staff and consulting psychologists, operated an individualised and outreach programme through a nationwide network of 23 centres and 150 teaching outposts inside and alongside schools, colleges and employment. We

* assessed 6,500 individuals
* taught 3,000 part-time (5-65 years)
* trained almost 5,000 teachers
* developed 850 D.I. Guild members through Dyslexia Review journal and Annual Symposium
* supplied information leaflets and support materials
* launched 3 'Understanding Dyslexia' videos – broadcast on television
* adapted Walter Bramley's literacy development programme 'Units of Sound' for CD Rom
* contributed to government consultations with a focus on improving literacy skills development for all children
* supported the teaching of 300 individuals financially.

The Dyslexia Institute, 133 Gresham Road, Staines TW18 2AJ
Tel: 01784 463851

Literacy and Dyslexia: Objectives for the Next Five Year

Introduction

Literacy and dyslexia are inextricably interwoven. Literacy is the ability to use words for informative and pleasurable reading and writing; dyslexic people have difficulty in learning how to use words.

Literacy underachievement is therefore the core effect of dyslexia. At least 7% of boys and 1% of girls are affected. Dyslexia creates one of the greatest provision challenges and causes of disagreement with parents in schools. Sadly, all too often it causes costly and difficult to remedy emotional, social and behavioural problems too.

It is the Dyslexia Institute's contention that resources may be wrongly focused because of inadequately rigorous literacy skills teaching for all, and poor understanding of dyslexia in many schools.

New research suggests that male and female brains process language differently; a challenge to teaching methods, with consideration needing to be given to separating boys and girls for literacy skills/English teaching.

Individual differences are relevant across the genders and between individual people who are shaped by genetics and their environment. All teachers need to understand these differences; specialist teachers need to be trained to develop the skills that are impeded in some children.

Parents have their part to play and IT can aid learning if used with focused software. Successful learning accompanies competence and confidence. Failure to acquire literacy skills, for whatever reason, leads to low self-esteem, challenging of 'the system' and all too frequently to wasted talent. How many *'excluded'* pupils also read and write badly? Too many, we suggest. It is our experience that improvement in behaviour results from the confidence and self-esteem that links with mastery of literacy skills and success in other curriculum areas.

Investment in good literacy teaching and identification of individual needs that leads, where necessary, to focused specialist teaching is clearly the way forward. With this strategy costs of failure and remediation should be reduced.

The Dyslexia Institute wants to help build a literate nation. In the next section we lay out six objectives to make this happen.

The Agenda for the next five years

Objective One: Training teachers effectively

To improve the initial and in-service training of all primary and secondary teachers in the understanding, assessment and development of literacy skills

- We believe that the emphasis should be on improving training in literacy skills teaching for all teachers, both primary and secondary, in initial teacher training and then as INSET for qualified teachers. This would reduce the failure of pupils in their early years at school and ensure that priority was given not only to developing early literacy skills but also to extending these skills to higher levels for study and work in secondary schools.

Objective Two: Using dyslexia expertise

To use teaching methods and materials originally created for dyslexic pupils to develop literacy skills more generally in schools

- Dyslexia specialists in Britain have developed literacy teaching principles, resources and systems that have as yet been largely un- tapped in helping to raise literacy standards not just for dyslexic pupils. The following are a few suggestions:

  - For young children materials such as *Letterland* are already used. Others such as Hornsby's *Before Alpha* could be used more widely

  - Key Stage 2, a more remedial approach could be provided by Walter Bramley's *Units of Sound* audio visual literacy develop- ment programme.

Objective Three: Resourcing individuals

To clarify the provision for the individual needs of *all* children and allocating resources in a more focused way.

In 1978 Baroness Warnock commented 'The purpose of education for all children is the same; the goals are the same. But the help that *individual* children need in progressing towards them will be different.'

The quality of the school learning environment can dramatically affect whether or not pupils succeed or fail. With the introduction of *Baseline Assessment* in 1997, and Records of Achievement throughout the school years, *Individual Education Plans* from Stage 2 of the *Code of Practice* on S.E.N. should be seen as a helpful way of managing the individual needs of pupils who need more help, including targeted teaching in a part-time withdrawal situation

Now surely is the time to embrace these individual needs; reallocating resources in a more imaginative way along the continuum from normal to the more specific, with focus on the vital early years leading to saving later.

Objective Four: Addressing gender issues

To consider the gender issue more fully and teach boys and girls appropriately.

In November 1996 Sally Shaywitz of Yale University School of Medicine reported, in Scientific American, that when brain function was observed by magnetic resonance imaging male and female brains responded differently to phonological processing. Men used only the left hemisphere of the brain, women used both sides. This is the first concrete proof of gender differences in the brain for any cognitive function and it could have significant implications for the teaching of boys and girls.

More boys than girls present for dyslexia assessment and teaching; the targeted teaching that proves successful for them could prove beneficial to boys generally.

Objective Five: Involving parents

To involve parents in learning about literacy skills development and give them confidence in helping their children and themselves.

- Children are shaped by their parents through genetics and environment

- Children who have literacy difficulties may well have parents who also had difficulties. Parents are anxious to avoid failure in their children and need to have confidence in the teaching profession

- Parents should be partners in helping to tackle literacy development but some may need help and guidance.

Objective Six: Using educational technology

To use technology to develop reading, spelling and writing in a systematic way.

- Computers organise, give practice and motivate. Expert teaching and good teaching materials can be enhanced with technological support. Word-processing is of clear benefit to all children. But we consider that greater clarity of purpose and quality of software content should be the focus of attention

- Integrated learning systems, for example, have benefits but currently fail to develop the core skills of decoding and structuring that are critical in literacy acquisition because existing software programmes do not address the problem adequately. Walter Bramley's *Units of Sound* on CDROM is an example of proven content and technical advances being used in combination.

Conclusion

The time has come to refocus thinking about dyslexia and to tackle the wider literacy issue using dyslexia expertise. All children need good literacy skills; all dyslexic children need to be taught literacy in a rigorous, structured, cumulative and multisensory way. The thrust of British education in the 1990s has been the raising of standards and achievement. It is of concern that universities still pose questions about the literacy skills of many students and that at the other end of the spectrum, there is a long tail of literacy underachievement – particularly in boys.

We have the skills and knowledge in Britain to build a literate nation; now we need a massive commitment to put a strategic agenda and key objectives into action.

22

Federation of Children's Book Groups

Penny Dolan

Chair 1996/1997

The Federation is a charity that aims to encourage the enjoyment and provision of books for children, and to inform any interested adults, especially parents, about children's books. It is an open organisation, run by volunteers, where parent and professionals such as teachers, librarians, booksellers, publishers etc. meet equally.

The main strength of the F.C.B.G. comes from various local Children's Book Groups, who organise meetings about children's books, including author visits. Some run family reading groups, storytimes in libraries, playschemes etc., or may help with local book provision. It holds an Annual Weekend and occasional One-day Conferences, promotes National Tell A Story Week, organises the Children's Book Award, and provides information about children's books. We welcome individual and professional membership.

Address: Federation of Children's Book Groups, 9 Westroyd, Pudsey, West Yorkshire LS28 8HZ. Tel: 0113 2579950.

Encouraging Children to be Part of the Reading Community

The Federation recognises that many important points about the development of literacy will be found in other entries within this publication. Therefore, this entry focuses on issues related most closely to the Federation.

Book Choice and Choice Books

Children will continue to need access to a wide range of books, and reading enjoyment should feature as highly as any curricular demands. Children need to be able to choose books that reflect their own image, and where they can explore other images – persons, places, cultures and histories, both 'real' and imaginary. They need a range of non-fiction books that balance content, illustration and text.

The individual child's choice, however, is more complex. Children do not always want to read widely. They become obsessive about certain texts, either as part of a peer-group passion, or on their own private journey. Reading may meet a child's needs in a side-long manner: when the pressures of life or school get too much, children may go for easy, familiar books instead. They may, often inspired by an adult's encouragement, try weightier books when they have 'room' for them. They read and re-read. Children's choices deserve respect, and books that speak to them at an individual level.

Book marketing practice, especially the rise of the series, has caused concern, but it is possible that various 'sensational' tales may close the reading gap, encouraging readers who would not otherwise be reading. Other books, given a 'series' look, may conceal diverse styles within similar covers. The real worry is whether all books should be expected to move sharply from shelf to till – the easy-reads pushing out quality writing. This practice, particularly in general or chain book-shops, is likely to restrict a wide choice of books. In a similar way, official lists of suggested texts may restrict both resourcing and reading opportunities. Young people's literacy is not helped by their being seen as consumers of blockbuster dump-bins, nor as analyse-the-plotline text-workers. Reading should offer enjoyment not just at 'fun' level, but real reader satisfaction.

The Federation, through the annual Children's Book Award, keeps this essential choice-within-books visible. Publishers can submit any titles. Many books circulate to many children around the U.K. Books are grouped into three categories – picture-book, shorter novel and longer novel. Favoured titles gradually emerge, are re-read, and the fifty 'Pick of the Year' books are chosen, listing titles enthusiastically read or heard by many children. This list also shows which titles were popular enough to be a 'Top Ten' book, and from this ten, children choose both the three category and the overall Children's Book Award winners.

The Children's Book Award stands for variety and for children's choice. We hope it will continue as a contribution to literacy in the future.

Informing the Reader

It is easy, if you work in a literacy-focused environment, to forget how hard it is for the ordinary parent to learn about children's books. Any literacy agenda should seek to promote real book awareness and information.

Information can be patchy. For example, children's book reviews flourish at Christmas and holiday time – as if no reading went on at other seasons. Publicity, rather than considered reading, may be behind a magazine review. So how does a parent make a balanced choice? Bookshops may not be supportive: shelves blocked with best-sellers, and no staff able to offer information or guidance. And the lay-out? How easy is it to get a push-chair through to the children's section of your local big bookshop? Should a Children's Access Award be on the literacy agenda?

Thankfully, some bookshops – especially the specialist children's book shops or departments – create welcoming environments, and some newspapers do review, or search out new ways to be involved with children's books. Recently, the Independent newspaper and Scholastic publishers have created the 'Story of The Year' anthology. Young Federation members now act as shortlist readers for this annual competition. Such good literacy news is, sadly, counterbalanced: changes in the children's library services, teacher-training and teacher-time affects knowledge about children's books. And, with the surge of child-care, do all involved with young children have good access to books and information about children's books? Doesn't the best literacy begin with babies?

The Federation is dedicated to sharing information about children's books. Book Groups offer regular discussions and talks. Annual Conferences, both Weekend and Day events, feature current authors, contemporary issues, and modern classics. Members receive a Newsletter and the excellent new 'Carousel' magazine. Federation Booklists, compiled by informed individuals around a theme or age group, select books from a whole range of publishers.

Young readers need to meet a wide range of books, but this selection is often in the care of the grown-ups. Informed opinion and understanding is vital for the future of literacy.

Being Part of the Reading Community

The junior reader needs particular encouragement. Opportunities for silent reading do not, alone, promote books. Literacy is encouraged by the energetic promotion of books, both individual texts and in general. In reading research, the D factor, 'drive', was always in the equation when considering the success of new learning materials. This drive, or energy, is still needed to fuel any literacy approaches. An enthusiastic teacher, or (better still) more than one, can improve the reading ethos of a whole school.

A positive image of literacy is important. Why do headlines never stress how many children are reading, or reading well, but only say how many aren't – as if children never pick this up? What about the self-fulfilling prophecy? We need to promote good news about reading, too.

Additionally, books don't open themselves. Even with adults, the thing that gets books opened – and read – is often external: the eager recommendation of a friend, or the hugely influential Book Circle network, or hearing an author talk. All this creates a special social energy. Children are no different (except that the wine-glass may be missing) in the need to feel part of the reading community.

A way of focusing this energy can be a good author visit. Local Children's Book Groups have often supported this need by assisting with arrangements for in-school visits or by children's writer or illustrator events open to the locality. The Federation is concerned that changes in various kinds of administration have made these more difficult. Regional Arts Boards support is limited, the Lottery is changing priorities in funding, and schools are finding it hard to justify such expenses. The Federation believes that such opportunities do help to build up a strong enthusiasm and ethos of literacy. They tell young children that reading is OK! The Federation's National Tell A Story Week in early May acts as a focus for many book events.

Finally

The Federation, as a small organisation, run by volunteers, is limited in what it can achieve in the current climate. Nevertheless, the Federation believes that the strength and goodwill of the many interested literacy organisations, if gathered together, can create an informed, positive environment, and an ethos that will let readers thrive, rather than shelter from a hail-storm of sound-bites and headlines.

23

The Library Association

Ross Shimmon

Chief Executive

The Library Association is the professional body for librarians and has over 25,000 personal members working in libraries of all types. It exists to promote the skills of librarians, encourage good practice and advocate the value of properly resourced library services to individual organisations and the nation as a whole. Our priorities are:

*   The Millennium bid to connect every public library to the information superhighway, which includes using the power of IT to support those needing help with literacy

*   National Libraries Week (November 1997), celebrating contribution of libraries to the nation. Children's libraries and lifelong learning are both themes of the week

*   Fighting for the adequate funding of our public and school libraries, one of the cornerstones in building a literate nation.

Address: The Library Association, 7 Ridgmount Street, London, WC1E 7AE
Tel: 0171 636 7543 Fax: 0171 436 7218

The Viewpoint of the Library Association

'Young people are going to need as much as ever the power to express themselves and the personal confidence to establish relationships which go with it. That means the power to handle words and concepts, whether in speech or writing, and the basis of that is the ability to read. To have learned to read once is not enough: it is as necessary to develop and retain the facility by constantly using it as it is to practise a foreign language. That means books and the familiarity with use of books which only access to a library can give.'

The words are those of Alan Bullock in his foreword to a government sponsored report on school libraries in 1984. Shamefully most of the recommendations in that report have not been acted upon despite the fact that it was called libraries 'the foundations of the curriculum'. Over ten years later another report, Investing in Children, could still comment on the widespread disparities in provision for children within schools and public libraries.

Literacy is the ability to read, along with the ability to spell and to write. It is the key skill that opens up the world of imagination, ideas and of intellectual debate. It is not only a skill crucial to personal development, but along with numeracy and IT skills, a vital life skill required for day-to-day living. It is also a skill that is necessary if an individual is to participate fully in society and make a contribution to the development and prosperity of that society. Therefore literacy is not only about the self-esteem and quality of life of individuals, important though those are, but it is also about the health and prosperity of society itself.

Libraries, especially school and public libraries, play an important role in promoting literacy. They do this at two stages. The first, and the one that must be got right for the sake of future generations, is that of encouraging and motivating the young learner. The second is by providing opportunities for adults who, for one reason or another, have not gained the reading skills necessary to participate fully in life.

Two factors have been acknowledged as key in encouraging the reading habit in children. The first is being read to at a young age by their parents or carers and the second is the constant provision of a wide range of high quality books. The public library, as the main provider of books for the under-fives, has a major responsibility in satisfying this need. Many public libraries already run imaginative Bookstart/Books for babies schemes designed to encourage parents to read to their children and introduce them to the pleasure of books. Others participate in family literacy projects where not only the needs of the child, but also any literacy problems faced by the parents can be solved in a sensitive fashion.

School libraries are important for the school-aged child and are normally supported by Schools Library Services centrally managed by the local education authority. School librarians are in a better position than most teaching staff to assess and meet the literacy needs of individual children as they see their use of the library and are able to monitor their use of books and other materials across all curriculum subjects. The public library offers supplementary provision and may well provide homework support and stimulate reading through reading clubs. Both school and public libraries will seek to increase children's enjoyment of reading through displays, literature-based activities within the library and work with publishers, writers and illustrators.

The Library Association is keen that all school and public libraries attain the standards of the best, so that all children have the opportunity to explore the world of imagination and ideas. We believe that local education authorities should be required by statute to provide a schools library service to support libraries in schools; that every secondary school should employ a chartered librarian to manage their library; and that every primary school should have access to the expertise of a chartered librarian. We are also keen that an assessment of the effectiveness of a school's library should become a key part of OFSTED inspections of schools. In respect of public libraries we have just published guidelines on public library services to children and young people which we hope will encourage good practice in all public library services.

The position of the adult with literacy problems is more sensitive. Librarians in FE Colleges and Adult Education Institutes already cater for students on Basic Skills courses and provide for students with varying levels of learning skills on other courses. However for many adults the public library is their only obvious source of help.

The public library service starts off with the advantage of a reputation for being welcoming and non-judgmental. Many libraries, normally in collaboration with other educational agencies, have open learning centres where basic skills learning materials can be found. There are a number of examples where individuals have overcome literacy problems and progressed to other educational achievements because of the public library. One winner of The Library Association's Independent Library Learner award started her learning as a member of a basic literacy course run with the help of library staff, and held in the library when it was closed. Perhaps more typically the public library provides materials and services relevant to the needs of adults but encourages them to make use of other specialist agencies for tutorial support.

These are some of the ways in which libraries can contribute to building a literate nation. However the statistics produced by the Basic Skills Agency continue to make depressing reading. It is clear there is still much to do. It is also clear that no single body can provide the whole answer and that, if the problem is to be tackled effectively, alliances have to form between all those concerned with the issue and a common agenda established. Perhaps then the issue would be less of a political football between the political parties and the necessary resources would be put into a co-ordinated effort to address the problem. The Library Association would be keen to cooperate in such a venture.

References

1. Library and information services council (England). *School libraries: the foundations of the curriculum.* HMSO, 1984. ISBN 011 630713 7

2. Library and information services council (England). *Investing in children: the future of library services for children and young people.* HMSO, 1995. ISBN 011 701994 1 National Association for the Teaching of English

3. *Children and young people: Library Association Guidelines for public library services,* 2nd edition. Edited by Catherine Blanshard. Library Association Publishing, 1997. ISBN 1 85604 209 X

24

National Association for the Teaching of English (NATE)

Anne Barnes

General Secretary

The National Association for the Teaching of English (NATE) is the UK subject teacher association for all aspects of English from pre-school to university. The association aims to support effective teaching and learning, to keep
teachers informed about current developments and to provide them with a
national voice.

The association is run on a voluntary basis through elected executive and
council committees. Members are affiliated to a network of regional and local
branches. The administrative base is in Sheffield where there are offices, a
meeting room, publication warehouse and dispatch centre.

The association has a range of committees and standing working parties
who address current concerns, disseminate knowledge and ideas, promote
the work of the association and seek to represent the views of the association to national bodies, local education authorities, the Department for
Education, Her Majesty's Inspector of Schools and examination boards.

In addition to our publications, which are written by teachers for teachers
with a view to spreading good ideas and information, we also feature quality
books on all aspects of English teaching.

We publish a journal 'English in Education', three times a year, which is
intended for all those professionally concerned with the learning and teaching
of English and drama in nursery, primary, secondary, further education and
higher education. It publishes articles, poems and reviews on all aspects of
English teaching, including drama, new technologies and media education.

Address: National Association for the Teaching of English, 50 Broadfield
Road, Broadfield Business Centre, SHEFFIELD S8 OXJ. Telephone: 0114 255
5419 Fax: 0114 255 5296 E-mail: nate.hq@campus.bt.com

NATE's view of the Strategic Agenda for Literacy over the Next Five Years

A strategic agenda for literacy over the next five years must:

- extend public conceptions of what it is to be literate in the last years of the twentieth century
- develop teachers' professionalism
- provide teachers and schools with the resources to do the job
- develop the links between schools and the wider community
- build a proper basis of information on children's developing literacy to inform teaching and curb the wild assertions of politicians and the press.

What it is to be literate in the last years of the twentieth century

Literacy is always relative. To be literate in the closing years of the twentieth century means something very different from being literate in the early nineteenth century. As we move towards the millennium, literacy must involve much more than the ability to lift words off the page (or screen), and to put them down. It must concern a confident experience of reading and 'writing' a wider range of texts for a wider range of purposes than our grandparents needed, or even dreamed of. This should include:

- texts from all over the English-speaking world, and, in translation, from further afield
- texts of argument and persuasion as well as information, narrative and poetry
- texts involving images as well as words
- TV and video texts
- computer texts including Interactive Multi Media.

Developing teachers' professionalism

Being a member of a profession involves making daily judgements in the light of a personal store of knowledge, developed partly through formal means and partly in the course of exercising that profession. In the years since the introduction of the national curriculum teachers' professionalism has been significantly eroded. Schools now have very little room to decide what is to be taught and are increasingly constrained as to the form that teaching takes. Official endorsement of an explicit didactic approach shapes the Ofsted's 'Three Boroughs' report (Ofsted, 1996a) and is set out in 'teacher proof' detail in the syllabus for schools caught up in the new Literacy Centre initiatives (Ofsted, 1996b).

Yet there is no one simple recipe for good literacy teaching. As Mortimore and Goldstein (1996) have pointed out, the argument in the 'Three Boroughs' report for didactic whole class teaching as the universal panacea is deeply flawed. Different classes in different parts of the country present different challenges. There is no one right way to teach literacy and no one right way to become a reader or writer. Good teachers have a rich view of what being literate means, an awareness of the materials and situations that can help children gain possession of such a literacy and the organisational and interpersonal skill to use these to productive effect.

For teaching of this quality to become the norm, an increased sense of professionalism is an essential element. If they are to enthuse children about literacy, provide them with materials that are encouraging and supportive, demonstrate what literacy is good for and how to go about it, guide children in what to read and what to look for in what they read, and assess their strengths, weaknesses and points of growth, teachers need much more than sets of instructions passed down from on high. They need to develop and refine their knowledge and understanding, and become increasingly reflective about what they do and why they do it.

One way in which this could be achieved would be to give more prominence to teacher assessment. A proper system of moderation should be set up, of the kind that was successful in ensuring parity of standards in the 100% coursework GCSE English syllabuses of the late eighties. The use of a framework such as the Primary Language Record (CLPE 1988) would greatly assist this process. The point is not to give teachers unlicensed freedom, but to give them a framework which encourages the development of knowledge, understanding and reflectiveness that improves the quality of judgement in the classroom.

The resources to do the job

If schools are to do a better job in promoting literacy, they need:

- texts
- computers
- space
- support.

If texts which children encounter in classrooms and school libraries are to compete with those they come across in the world outside, schools will need considerably more money. But if the school texts lack the visual appeal and modernity of those they see on the street, in the newsagent and in their homes, school literacy will seem of marginal importance to many.

Equipping classrooms with the computers to give all children experience of composing on a word-processor and of using interactive multi-media is not going to be cheap. But if we fail to do so, and fail to train teachers in teaching children to use this technology, we risk creating an even bigger divide between those who see computers as good only for playing games and those whose homes have given them a confident command of the literacies of the age.

Schools need space to ensure that libraries are more than converted cloakrooms, to enable reading and writing to be given significant permanent areas in primary classrooms and to allow dramatic representation to take its proper place in bringing existing texts to life and creating new texts.

If teachers are to become more professional and to devote themselves more fully to the literacy needs of their pupils, they will need classes small enough to make this possible and non-teaching support ranging from the qualified nursery nurse in reception to qualified librarians and IT technicians in secondary school.

Developing links with the wider community

In the majority of primary schools there is now a home-school partner-ship scheme which ensures that in Key Stage 1 at least, children regularly take books home to read with their parents. As well as ensuring that this practice becomes universal, we now need to make it more truly collabora-tive, so that the parents are seen as real partners, with important informa-tion and insights to contribute to their children's teachers.

And the notion of the texts, literacies and community need to be extended. All too often the literacy purveyed in school has little to do with the life of the community outside. Children and parents need to see that schools recognise the literacies that are of significance in their communities, from reading the mail order catalogue to writing the letter about housing bene-fit. Schools also need to recognise different ways of approaching such texts, and not measure every literacy practice in terms of some middle class norm.

Assessment and monitoring

Teachers and parents need to know where their children are and how to help them forward. Government at all levels and the population at large need to know how we stand in our literacy teaching. At the moment we have an enormously cumbersome system which is intended to provide all this, but succeeds in doing none of it properly. The current apparatus pays too little attention to teachers' educated and disciplined perceptions, and fails to encourage a thoroughly formative approach. We need a system of formative assessment that takes into account:

• children's ideas and feelings about their literacy learning

• how individual children go about their reading and writing

• parents' perceptions of the process; and that orients teachers towards making use of this information in planning future teaching and learn-ing. The Primary Language Record provides us with a sound basis for such assessment.

In addition, we need a national monitoring system, operating through light sampling, that as well as telling us how our children are doing in constructing meaning from test passages, also gives us information about:

- what children read – including a range of computer texts as well as poetry, picture books, other fiction and texts concerned to inform, persuade and argue in conventional print

- how much they read and how much they like reading

- what they make of what they read – how they relate what's in the text to what they know from experience and encountering other texts. We need similar information about their writing.

25
National Library for the Blind

Ilene Hoyle, National Library for the Blind and
Steve McCall, Birmingham University

The National Library for the Blind is the largest Braille and Moon library resource in Western Europe. With stocks of over 350,000 volumes, we cater for the reading needs of nearly 5,000 individuals who read by touch.

Our library extends from contemporary fiction to the classics, from Booker Prize winners to Delia Smith's cookery books, from biography to up to date travel guides. We have 7,500 scores of braille music. Book lists are tailored to individual needs. A range of catalogues is available, including a new children's catalogue supplement.

Ours is a totally free postal lending library. We post roughly 1,000 volumes to our readers each day, and the same number are returned. Freepost Articles for the Blind ensures that our books travel by first class post, and whether readers are on the Isle of Skye or Penzance, they receive their books by return of post.

We encourage and promote reading and literacy, through embossed literature, and we can support teachers and learners with specific requirements or resource needs. We stock material to help new readers. We are keen to ensure that students of Braille and Moon have the tools they need to become literate in the embossed code of their choice.

Address: National Library for the Blind, Cromwell Road, Bredbury, Stockport SK62SG

Tel: 0161 494 0217 Fax: 0161 406 6728

Literacy Through Touch

For almost two hundred years a major concern for those involved in the education and welfare of people who are blind has been the promotion of literacy and for one hundred of those years the NLB has been at the forefront of the development of promoting literacy through touch.

Braille

The first efforts to develop a systematic tactile reading code were based upon reproducing the letters of the print alphabet in a raised form. Many raised line versions of the print alphabet were produced but they proved of limited value, mostly because the sighted people who invented them paid more attention to the appearance rather than the feel of the letters.

It was a blind man, Louis Braille, who invented the code that has become the universal medium of touch readers. Braille's system was developed from a rectangular block of six equally spaced dots arranged in two columns of three. This six dot pattern is known as a cell. By taking the dots singly and in patterns it is possible to form sixty-three different combinations. These are used to represent letters, groups of letters known as 'contractions', whole words, numbers, punctuation and other print symbols (see page opposite). Although Braille had perfected his code by 1834, it was not adopted in France until after his death and did not become widely used in Britain until fifty years after its invention. Braille has now been adapted to most languages and there are many specialist braille codes including ones for mathematics, music and science. It can be easily written through a variety of methods of which the oldest involves the use of a slate and stylus.

Standard English braille is in two grades: Grade 1 which contains no contractions, and Grade 2 which uses 189 contractions. The vast majority of books for touch readers are published in Grade 2 braille.

In 1882 NLB began with 50 books in a front room. Current stocks exceed 350,000 braille volumes.

Moon

Only one other tactile code has survived from the plethora of systems invented in the last century. The Moon code (called after its English inventor the Reverend William Moon) was developed in 1847. Until the advent of braille, Moon was Britain's most popular touch reading system. Moon is a line based code in which many of the letters are simplified versions of letters in the alphabet.

Moon has survived to this day as an alternative to braille, being used mostly by the elderly blind who lack the sensitivity of touch to manage braille. It has recently enjoyed a revival and research is being undertaken at the University of Birmingham into its suitability for children for whom braille is inappropriate.

NLB houses the largest collection of Moon in the world.

Literacy

The literacy of people who are blind continues to be a subject of concern for those involved in the education and rehabilitation of the blind. A 1991 survey undertaken by the Royal National Institute for the Blind (RNIB) estimated that there are 757,000 people with visual impairments who live in private households. Of these people around 300,000 have a visual impairment sufficiently severe for them to be registerable as blind. The survey showed that only around 19,000 of these people have learnt braille well enough to read a braille magazine or a book. Of these 13,000 remain active readers while 10,000 write in braille. The number of Moon readers has been estimated at less than a thousand.

It would be easy to conclude from these startling figures that braille is a skill of minor importance to people who are blind, that it is an irrelevant activity that is in decline, perhaps a victim of advances in technology which will soon render it completely obsolete. But such conclusions would be wrong.

Blindness is most commonly a condition associated with old age. 90% of the people in the survey who were registerable as blind were over 60. Clearly there is enormous work to be done in promoting touch reading among the elderly blind, but if one concentrates on the 17,000 people between the ages of 16 and 59 who are registered as blind, a totally different picture of the importance of braille emerges. 81% of people of employable age have been taught braille and although only 6,000 people who are registered blind are in paid employment, half of the blind people who do have jobs use braille in the workplace. Clearly mastery of braille significantly enhances employment prospects.

The need for embossed literature

There is no evidence either that demand for instruction in braille is in decline. The RNIB compared the results of its survey with those of an earlier survey taken in 1965 and found that there had been a proportional increase in braille readership among the registered blind in the 16-59 age range. While 33% of registered blind in 1965 had never learned braille, by 1986 this figure had dropped to only 19%.

Another rumour about braille is that it will be made obsolete by advances in technology. This has been a popular misconception for at least three decades. The advent of tape recorders in the 1960s led some educators to conclude that the widespread availability of information on tape would mean that children would no longer need to be taught to read through braille. This belief proved disastrous for the education of some blind children in the USA.

Braille has many advantages over tape or synthetic speech as a medium. Crucially braille provides the reader with hard copy, enabling the reader to control and vary the pace of assimilation according to the complexity of the material. It is an active rather than a passive process in which the braille reader has complete control, reviewing or scanning the text as required.

Fully sighted people can now access books through tape and compact disc and access newspapers and journals through the Internet, but there is no suggestion that this will do away for the need for hard copy. Like most sighted people, people who are blind want a choice of media for accessing print.

Braille and Technology

Contrary to popular belief, advances in technology are likely to serve to increase the availability of braille in the next five years. Computer programmes which can quickly translate print files into Grade 1 or Grade 2 braille for downloading to braille embossers are now widely available at affordable prices for all types of desktop computers. With additional equipment costing a few hundred pounds, it is easy to produce text in braille for a blind customer or employee as it is to produce print for a sighted customer or employee.

Legislation too is likely to increase the amount of braille available to people who are blind. The Disability Discrimination Act lays an obligation on employers to provide information in an accessible form for customers and employees who are blind. For many people who are blind this preferred form will be braille.

The threats to reading through touch then are not the ones that are commonly held. But the threats are real. They reside in the shortage of professionals with the competence or the time to teach blind adults who want to learn braille or Moon. They reside in the lack of research into the best methods of teaching tactile codes to adults. They reside in attitudes that regard literacy for people who are blind as an amenity rather than a right.

The future for the National Library for the Blind

The agenda for the National Library for the Blind over the next five years is to increase the readership of people who use braille and Moon by

- promoting public awareness of the importance of touch reading
- supporting the training of teachers of braille and Moon
- commissioning and supporting relevant research into touch reading
- organising national conferences on aspects of literacy through touch.

The Library will continue to serve the needs of existing touch readers through efficient and responsive provision of specialist library services into the next century.

26
National Literacy Association

Charlie Griffiths

Project Director '99 by '99 Campaign

The National Literacy Association aims to ensure that, when they leave school, 99% of children will have adequate literacy for their needs in daily life. NLA is an 'umbrella' organisation with an Executive Committee largely made up of the representatives of other educational organisations, including five teachers' unions. Although NLA campaigns for a greater awareness of the needs of children who habitually under-achieve, we also work to put our words into action. NLA runs the Docklands Learning Acceleration Project which is the biggest primary school literacy and technology project in the country. The Project works with over six hundred 7 and 8 year olds to raise standards and expectations of children's literacy. The Project uses the latest in multi-media and portable technology as well as more traditional methods to motivate children at school and to involve their families at home.

Address: National Literacy Association, 5 Airspeed Road, Priory Industrial Park, Christchurch, Dorset BH23 4HD. Tel: 01425 272232

NLA Docklands Learning Acceleration Project : Tel 0171 537 1329

Practical Strategies for the Next Five Years

As we approach the millennium, our nation is looking to the next century with hope and anticipation of a bright, new future: less poverty, less crime, greater security – jobs, homes and a loving environment – for everyone. Simple aspirations which, in a civilised modern society hovering on the edge of the 21st century should already be the reality. If it is ever to be so, the first step towards that 'Utopia' must be to ensure that our children and young people are equipped with the literacy skills demanded by the society of today and, even more so, of tomorrow.

Every year 16% of school-leavers, approximately 100,000, leave school with inadequate literacy. Since the start of universal state education, the percentage of young people with poor literacy has remained much the same. This has led, I believe, to a general acceptance, almost resignation, that because we've always had this number with poor literacy, then we always will; that there are certain children who just cannot or will not learn the basic skills of reading, writing and spelling. This simply isn't so. I don't think any child goes to school not wanting to learn, not wanting to keep up with the others in the class. So, when a child starts having problems with learning, it is not due to their 'not trying', 'daydreaming', being 'lazy' or 'deliberately difficult' – just some of the reasons often put forward for a child's difficulties. The vast majority of children CAN learn to read and write adequately but literacy is a skill like any other; some pick it up with ease no matter what method of teaching is being used, others may need a little extra help to acquire it. We have to look at the individual child and say 'What will work for that child?' and respond accordingly. This will invariably cost money but it is surely much more cost-effective to invest in education so that children leave school literate and employable, than to support a host of disillusioned and disheartened young people who can't get jobs, many of whom will end up turning to crime.

At the National Literacy Association, we believe that one of the most important factors influencing children's ability to achieve is our expectations of them. If we expect them to fail, then they will no see no point in trying; if we expect them to achieve, then they will strive for success. There are too many children of whom our expectations are so low that they are virtually 'written off' before they've even started – children of single mothers, children from inner-cities, children in care, children from certain cultural backgrounds, children with certain disabilities. Yes, these children do have disadvantages to overcome, but their biggest hurdle of all is the way we pre-judge and stereotype them.

Many children are caught in a spiral of low-achievement and lack of purpose. They look around them and see high-levels of unemployment, adults who never read – perhaps can't read – and they see no purpose in education and little that has any bearing on their daily lives. If we are to achieve a more literate society, then we must break this cycle of failure and recognise that it is not the children who are failing, but we who are failing them.

So what are the practical strategies we, at the National Literacy Association, would like to see put in place?

Expectation

- The National Literacy Association is committed to ensuring that, when they leave school, 99% of children will have adequate literacy for their needs in daily life. NLA believes this should be set as a national target by the Government by 1999, so that, as a country, we raise our expectations of what children *can and will* achieve. Anything less than this presupposes that our society expects a significant percentage of the population to be functionally illiterate. This cannot be acceptable.

Teaching and the school environment

- Teachers need and want better training on the teaching of reading and writing skills both during their Initial Teacher Training and during In-Service Training. Teachers need to be familiar with and able to use a variety of teaching approaches. They also need to be able to identify at an early age those children whose literacy difficulties are caused by dyslexia and other specific learning difficulties so that those children can have access to the appropriate help and resources. We need to emphasise the centrality of literacy i.e. that without the basics of reading and writing, the whole curriculum is inaccessible. Literacy must be seen as the responsibility of all teachers, irrespective of subject speciality, and not just the domain of the Class Teacher, English teacher or the Special Needs teacher.

• There should be specific training on how to work with parents and other carers and involve them in their children's learning and in the life of the school

• Teachers, especially Primary Teachers, have too little flexibility because of the National Curriculum requirements. The curriculum should serve the needs of the child and not vice versa

• We would like to see a major re-think on class size so that the youngest children have the smallest class sizes

• Schools need more books!

  • Text Books: EVERY child should have access to their OWN set of text books for use at home and at school. Sharing one book between three pupils is NOT effective and should not be acceptable or accepted

  • Reading for Pleasure: There needs to be an increase in books in the class and in school libraries. This means increasing the budget for books and targeting a certain minimum percentage of the budget for spending on books. Schools should not have to make a choice between a new roof or more books.

Information Technology

• Government should take a lead in advocating the new methods of educating children i.e. the use of IT. Times are changing fast, but schools aren't able to keep up

• The biggest hindrance to the effective use of IT in schools is lack of training and support for teachers. Teachers need to be introduced to the benefits of IT during their Initial Teacher Training and specific training on IT should be available to ALL teachers at all stages of their career

- Within five years, every school-age child and every teacher should have access to portable computer technology for use in the class and at home

- Information and training on IT should be offered to parents and carers so that they can take an active interest in their children's learning and improve their own basic and IT skills. This could be done through community-based projects centred on the school. (The NLA Docklands Learning Acceleration Project already offers an accredited training scheme and we are seeing some very significant benefits).

Parents, carers and the home environment

- Appropriate state-supported nursery education should be available to all children from the age of three and means-tested assistance with child-care for children under that age. This does have a direct bearing on literacy because so often families and in particular single mothers are caught in the poverty trap; they would like to work but can't because the cost of child care is prohibitive. Poverty means disheartened and stressed-out parents who certainly don't have money for books. FREE nursery education for all 3 year olds would, at the very least, ensure some exposure to books and stories before school

- We would like to see a National Parental/Carer Accreditation Scheme set up giving credit for a range of literacy activities such as sharing books, learning new skills with their child, helping in school, learning IT skills with their child etc

- VAT should NEVER be put on children's books

- As books in the home are such an important influence, we would like to see Government support for a number of initiatives encouraging an early introduction to books and 'shared reading' – such as The Book Trust's 'Book Start' Project and NLA's Bounty Pack for New Mothers Scheme

* Information and training should be available to Health Visitors and other medical professionals on identifying early speech and language difficulties which could be an indication of later difficulties with reading and writing. In addition we would like to see an increase in the number of Speech and Language Therapists.

If all or even some of these objectives were achieved within the next five years, this would, indeed, be a major step towards a more literate society; a society better equipped to deal with and take advantages of the changes, challenges and opportunities that will be part of the 21st century; a society whose young people have a sense of worth and purpose, who can contribute to and partake of our social and economic well-being.

It would be naive if we thought this could be achieved without increasing the budget for education. Any Government which is going to ensure a more literate nation must be prepared to invest in it. But the long term benefits will far outweigh the short term costs. After all, to quote Cicero 'What greater gift or better can we offer to the State than if we teach and train up youth?'.

27
National Literacy Trust

Neil McClelland

Director

The National Literacy Trust was established in October 1993. Its main purposes are:

* to work with others to enhance literacy standards in the UK

* to encourage more reading and writing for pleasure by children, young people and adults

* to raise the profile of the importance of literacy in the context of social and technological change.

Our major work to date includes:

* the establishment of a national literacy database and information service

* the publication of a quarterly journal, *Literacy Today*

* contributions to national policy debates and developments

* the development of a 'literacy collaborative' model, which is being launched initially in Newcastle

* the establishment of Reading Is Fundamental, UK

* support to a number of literacy initiatives and local education authorities.

National Literacy Trust, Swire House, 59 Buckingham Gate, London, SWIE 6AJ

Tel: 0171 828 2435 Fax: 0171 931 9986 E-mail: literacytrust@org.uk.

Creating a New Climate – Collaboration for Literacy

The National Literacy Trust is delighted that literacy is being accorded a higher priority in educational, economic and political debates. We believe that the achievement of enhanced literacy skills and the encouragement of wider participation in literacy activities should be critical objectives for our nation. Since our launch we have argued that we have a serious literacy gap in the UK, and that the solution will require, amongst other things: an even higher priority for literacy in our schools; finding new ways to unlock more parental support; and an acceptance that the achievement of world class literacy standards will require a systematic and concerted whole community approach.

We are pleased that we have made a contribution to the raised profile of literacy. However we are worried about the tendency to look for easy solutions to complex issues surrounding learning in our society. Whilst the majority of children are well taught in good schools and achieve highly satisfactory levels of literacy, there is no room for complacency. There are children and adults who require immediate and effective support and there are also important strategic imperatives. These can only be delivered through cool and objective analysis followed by investment and change. The fact that so many adults have inferior literacy skills is a national embarrassment and a phenomenal waste for each individual and for society.

Although many children are now acquiring more impressive literacy skills than did generations of children in the past, it is likely that the number of children who are not properly equipped either for secondary school or the world of work is increasing. Ultimately we reap what we sow and our response to both the urgent individual needs and the longer term strategic issues must reflect the need to avoid quick-fix solutions – there are no short-cuts – no panaceas. The 'fix the schools', 'fix the parents' bandwagons are simplistic and therefore distorting. Such negativity and blaming is counterproductive and we need to operate in a more positive way.

So what should a strategic agenda to address the nation's literacy needs consist of? Many contributions to this book deal in detail with the school sector issues and so, for the purposes of this contribution, we have concentrated on the wider community and parental dimensions.

• Firstly, as a nation, we should accept that while high quality teaching is essential, it is not sufficient. Schools operate in a social context and we must find ways to ensure that the wider culture is more supportive of the teaching and learning process.

The role of schools is critical. We must accord primary teaching a higher status; resource primary schools better – class sizes are increasing; give more time to literacy and recognise that early intervention is necessary and cost effective. The benefits of such approaches as 'Reading Recovery', 'Success for All' and 'First Steps' need to be thoroughly examined. We need to get it right first time.

However, the whole community must be involved. The Trust's view is that we need to develop literacy in this country by planning systematically across four dimensions. We have defined these as: **Inner strand** – formal education; **Outer strand** – the home and the various communities and cultures surrounding formal education; **Supply side** – the quality and quantity of the offered or supplied literacy teaching experiences and support; and the **Demand side** – the creation, by inner and outer strand activity, of the confidence, motivation and demand for literacy in each individual, pupil or adult; the extent to which each wants to be engaged in literacy. We need to generate new collaborations across all four dimensions.

And we have to search for immediate and for long term strategies to 'market' literacy for both achievement and enjoyment. However unorthodox, we need to find the motivators that generate a demand for involvement and achievement – particularly for the many young people who are not sufficiently motivated by conventional educational approaches. This we believe is a critical and undervalued in the current debate. Involving professional footballers in our national poster campaign and in Reading Is Fundamental has been effective and we need to build on this approach. There is a need to harness partnerships across society to 'sell' the importance and pleasure of reading and writing to young people and, given the evidence of underachievement, particularly to boys and young men.

There is a clear, but not inevitable, correlation between achievement and economic disadvantage, and schools serving communities with high levels of poverty undoubtedly have to face additional pressures. Nonetheless, we should resolve that all children can and must learn, and so respond more effectively and imaginatively if children come to school less able to give of their best. We must examine why some children and some schools are doing so well despite unpromising circumstances.

- Parental involvement is crucial and we have to build on and disseminate the work of schools that have found ways to make parents feel **needed** in the partnership for children's literacy development.

To stress the importance of parents and the home is nothing new. However, we believe that an urgent and concerted national campaign is needed to support the home and encourage more parental confidence and involvement. No parents should feel, as some undoubtedly do, that they are not, or cannot become, sufficiently skilled to make a significant contribution to their children's literacy development. Positive messages need to be persuasively communicated to all parents, and we require the communities of business, the media, the health sector and the arts to work together with us on this. The messages must include the obligations of the home; all parents should find time every day to read to or with their children.

As part of a strategy we should be prepared to fund experimental methods for supporting parents of 0-2 year olds to become more confident and better equipped for their role in the early language and literacy support of their children.

- We know that enhanced parental involvement and inter-generational literacy approaches are successful, so more family literacy initiatives should be established.

- Systematic and co-ordinated ways to involve substantially more volunteers to work for literacy are a priority. Volunteers can perform many roles, from supporting adult basic education students through to school-based one-to-one work with children with reading difficulties. Volunteers would not replace the work of qualified teachers but can be a profoundly important complement. A national campaign to encourage volunteering for literacy could be highly effective.

- We must think strategically and analytically and ensure that we evaluate and spread good practices effectively – so that the education system can be quickly informed about new initiatives and outcomes. This is the work the Trust is developing through its database and information service.

- The Trust's position is that high quality literacy standards require a great deal more than the acquisition of basic skills. These are of course the critical foundations but we must also light up the imagination, confidence and motivation of our children so that each has a life-long desire to be involved in more extended literacy practices. Otherwise their basic skills may begin to deteriorate and so become inadequate for secondary school, work or society. In some ways, this creation of an inner demand within each pupil and student for continuing and extended participation in literacy is the biggest challenge of all.

- Finally we advocate that, with imaginative leadership from the Government, we should make a national commitment to place literacy as the pre-eminent educational goal for the next five years. This will require a national strategy that includes literacy for both functional and more intrinsic and recreational purposes. It will require a perspective on literacy development that recognises the key roles of our schools and the need continually to enhance the skills of teachers, as well as the importance of the wider learning that takes place outside of formal education and the influence of the culture created by the media and others. All local education authorities should be expected to draw up strategic plans for literacy, incorporating partnership links with key local interests such as Training and Enterprise Councils, libraries, arts, health, local media and which, consistent with a national framework, should be particular to the local circumstances of each community.

As we said at the establishment of the National Literacy Trust, we need a 'Crusade for literacy' – a ten year crusade that will be inclusive, entirely positive, systematically conducted – with clarity of goals and shared aspirations – and which articulates a broad-based concept of literacy. We can stimulate the national imagination and will to transform literacy in our country. The social and economic benefits will be immense.

28
Northern Ireland Adult Literacy and Basic Education Committee (ALBEC)

Hilary A. Sloan
Chairperson

ALBEC

* promotes, encourages and reviews all aspects of basic education for adults, including literacy and numeracy; maintains links with other bodies with similar interests; promotes quality standards in the delivery of basic education.

Major recent achievements

* advisory papers produced for Department of Education (NI) on Incorporation; better targeting of publicity; a celebratory day on 7 September 1996 where adult literacy students from all over Ireland took to the stage and made the day theirs.

Priorities

* to raise the status of ABE/Adult Literacy; to keep in mind the broad remit of 'literacy' for the whole society; to develop partnerships.

Future programme

* networking; policy influencing; more provision for students' voices to be heard.

Address: ALBEC, 344 Stranmillis Road, BELFAST BT9 5ED
Telephone:: 01232 682 379

The Strategic Agenda for Literacy in Northern Ireland

The Northern Ireland Adult Literacy and Basic Education Committee (ALBEC) is a sub-committee of the Northern Ireland Council for Adult Education and comprises people with a deep concern for, and many years experience in, literacy work. Such a group has been in existence for the last twenty years in a co-ordinating and monitoring role. Despite growth in the main area of adult education over the last ten years there has not been comparable growth in adult basic education/literacy. This deficit has not really been explored as no major piece of research into the reasons why so few people have come forward for help has been carried out to date.

Literacy is wider than just 'basic skills'. The whole functional approach as outlined by government in their consultation document, Lifelong Learning, 5.1 – 'Basic skills are the ability to read, write and speak English and to use mathematics at a level necessary for work and society in general' does not represent the needs of the broad spectrum of people. The definition of literacy must go beyond the confines of the government's statement in order to include literacy for personal development and literacy for enjoyment and the image of literacy under which some students may feel stigmatised must change.

Literacy for all does not just mean those who can and will get a job; it must help to promote the social inclusion of those who for whatever reasons are at the margins of economic and social life. Many people today have been displaced because of the economic situation and the change in the industrial structure leading to the need for a high degree of technological knowledge. Literacy needs to push out its boundaries into this area as well whether it is labelled retraining or relearning. If literacy, therefore, is to be part of the national agenda it must form a central part of each organisation's strategic plan. Only through this mechanism will it be recognised as being a fundamental element of student learning support, attracting appropriate resources.

ALBEC would therefore put forward *seven* areas where careful strategic planning needs to take place in Northern Ireland:

• Good research/evaluation into (i) the different motivations of people seeking help in reading/writing, (ii) good practice where it exists, (iii) the actual numbers of people who need help and (iv) the reasons which keep people from seeking help

• Accreditation should be available for all those who require it; however, this should be accompanied by the recognition that all learners do not necessarily seek accreditation for their learning outcomes. The process of setting targets in literacy must be approached with sensitivity and caution. There is evidence to suggest that where the promotion of literacy is linked to forms of assessment or competencies there is often a negative outcome

• The lack of literacy skills must not cause people to be doubly disadvantaged when using modern technology. There must be equality of access to technology e.g. the information superhighway, word-processing

• Those involved in future planning for literacy must never overlook people with special needs e.g. those with special learning needs, travellers, ex-offenders, unemployed adults

• The training of trainers – the future role of FE may not be in the actual delivery to every student (other people in future may take over this role) but FE should have a major role in training and the provision of good backup resources. However, this can involve considerable staff development cost and this cost must not be overlooked when strategies are being discussed

• The development of partnerships e.g. (i) the partnership between the FE colleges and the community through the Family Literacy programme which does target socially marginalised groups; (ii) the development of literacy programmes in co-operation with employers, thereby linking in to the themes of 'Investing in People' and 'Lifelong Learning'

- The provision of a co-ordinating body for ABE/ Literacy – a body with adequate funding and the ability to lobby independently where necessary (cf. BSA in England/Wales or NALA in the Republic of Ireland).

Adequate funding underpins all these areas and it is vital if we are to build a literate nation which includes all communities.

The goal-posts of literacy are changing. A new approach does not mean that all of the old approach is abandoned; literacy must be embedded in the whole notion of a learning society with access at different points to meet differing needs. This is vital, especially in Northern Ireland, as there is no possibility of people playing their part in moving this society forward in peace and reconciliation if they are lacking the necessary literacy skills.

The publication of the consultative document on Lifelong Learning by the Department of Education for Northern Ireland and the impending publication of draft legislation on Incorporation in FE Colleges offers ALBEC an opportune time to put forward its strategic agenda for the next five years. The opportunity must be grasped to redefine literacy as a fundamental human right rather than a target to be met.

29

The Poetry Society

Alison Combes

Education Development Officer

In 1909 The Poetry Society was established to promote poets and poetry in the United Kingdom. It campaigns for poetry wherever possible and aims to develop Britain's outstanding tradition of poetry by supporting our new poets today.

The Society's work includes publishing 'Poetry Review', Britain's best-selling poetry magazine and 'Poetry News', the Society's quarterly newsletter to members.

The education department co-ordinates the W.H. Smith's Poets In Schools scheme and Poetry in Health placements.

The Society publishes a variety of poetry packs for primary and secondary school children.

It co-ordinates events for National Poetry Day and runs The National Poetry Competition. The Society provides a national information service on poets, events, festivals, competitions and gives advice on a range of subjects.

Address: The Poetry Society, 22 Betterton Street, LONDON WC2H 9BU. Telephone: 0171 240 4810 Fax 0171 240 4818

E-mail poetrysoc@dial.pipex.com

Literacy Towards the Millennium

Although it may be difficult, I should like us to forget the millennium for a moment. Unlike the poets of the nineteenth century, the Poetry Society is not yet suffering from those fin de siecle blues. Not only are there another three years to go before the year 2000, but at the time of writing in the UK , another general election looms. As always, given the lack of easy promises to be made about the economy, this has led to a renewed interest in education being expressed by politicians of all parties and at all levels. New technologies and nursery provision have both taken a recent turn centre stage whilst security issues – in the wake of the deaths at Dunblane and the murder of Philip Lawrence – have been a rightful concern. Yet as always it is the matter of standards which predominates. In the education press, literacy is the issue of the moment and debate regarding the programme soon to be implemented in the DFEE's new literacy centres is rife. Politicians, parents and educationalists all have their own ideas about the potential benefits and shortcomings of this programme. The same interest groups also have their own plans regarding how the cause of universal literacy might be advanced in Britain. Most of the schemes which they envisage are sophisticated, all-embracing, long-term and expensive. No such grandiose schemes will be delineated here – I wouldn't claim to have the necessary expertise – but then the modest changes advocated in this document could be put in place and begin to take effect long before the millennium arrives. Already the Arts Council of England's new *Arts for Everyone* initiative could make the monies required available to all schools and youth consortia at least.

Yet at a time when functional literacy is a major concern – when the Secretary of State for Education has launched her own *Better English Campaign* with a view to enhancing the practical communication skills of those first entering the job market – and when the Labour Party's commitment to the new technologies is predicated upon the premise that all workers will be system users who must be able to read – why should schools worry about the role of arts education in reading acquisition? What contribution might a poet make towards the skilling of technologists for the next millennium? Surely the need to consider the artistic/poetic content of any literacy programme would be an undue pressure for the nation's teachers who already battle at the chalkface to overcome basic problems of functional literacy and numeracy?

As always the question of meaningful communication is crucial. Although the Labour Party's concern for the use of new technologies in the classroom is timely at the point where growth of communication systems such as the Internet is exponential, it would appear that – here as abroad – concern to date has focused entirely on the superstructure (cabling, access to the information superhighway; computer hardware): on the medium rather than the message. Politically, this preoccupation may be understandable in the run-up to an election. Practically, of course, hardware has to be provided first. Educationally, however, such exclusive preoccupations must always cause concern. They are certainly a matter for consideration now as the first computer packages designed to facilitate reading acquisition come on-line. So far, most of the packages available have been designed in the United States. The quality of both their production and design might best be described as patchy – although the computerised version of Sesame Street is predictably good. Further along the developmental range, when studying literature in depth rather than trying to acquire basic reading skills, sophisticated packages which demonstrate the potential of this medium, like the BBC's *Macbeth* on CD-ROM, do exist. Inspired by such examples, the Poetry Society has already become involved in researching and developing literature education projects at the cutting edge: developing a virtual *Poetry Place* for education projects for the Internet and producing occasional teaching packs available on paper and via the world-wide-web. Certainly, as an arts agency involved in advocacy and development of the artform, the Poetry Society interest is in conveying meaningful messages to young readers which will encourage them to develop existing skills by reading further – whatever the medium.

However, due to the complexities inherent in their production, computer packages are usually expensive for a parent or a classroom teacher and besides, in order to operate any of the reading acquisition programmes to full advantage, a sound card is required – which may mean you have to update your hardware before you can run your new package. Undoubtedly, as integrated learning project like *Pen Down* in Somerset and that recently run by the LDDC in London's Docklands reveal, the use of new technologies and related reading programmes can result in significantly improved scores on standardised attainment tests. Yet as the *Pen Down* report concluded, these products are actually much less effective when learners use them unsupervised – as much of their final success appears dependent on the increased incidence and defined nature of individual or small group interaction with their teachers in the classroom. In other words, these projects would seem to operate much as a reading recovery programme does and in these instances, the computer *currently* appears to be little more than a glamorous accessory. Of course, better-designed interactive reading programmes, which offer something more than the ubiquitous *cloze* activities, must appear as we learn to evaluate and then to exploit the multi-sensory potential of this new medium to the full advantage of would-be readers. Undoubtedly, literature too will change in response to changes in the way that people acquire basic reading skills – and the Poetry Society will witness the advent of various new forms of poetry.

However, it is worth bearing in mind, while such projects are still in the first stages of development, we can already bring a multi-sensory approach to reading acquisition much more cheaply into schools. For a verbal artist will almost certainly utilise a variety of sensory stimuli when working with children. Not only will s/he talk to a group whilst showing its members words in a story of her own creation, s/he may use pictures or music to reinforce a particular message or inspire imaginative work. That verbal artist does not usually require you to upgrade your computer hardware in order to function in your learning environment and s/he can usually work with a whole class (rather than the 2 or 3 who work at a computer) at once. Given the importance of structured human interaction to the success of projects such as *Pen Down* and reading recovery programmes, what might the value of sustained interaction with a practising verbal artist, who must by definition have more sophisticated communication skills than most, turn out to be?

More seriously, recent research by psycholinguists would seem to demonstrate concrete reasons for the use of verbal arts in early years education.

The connections between nursery rhymes and speech acquisition were first posited long ago and have been studied by writers as diverse as Julia Kristeva and Iona Opie whilst the Celtic bards were well aware that the use of rhythm and rhyme in speech aids memory. Now studies by Usha Goswami sponsored by Oxford University Press provide a more sophisticated theoretical frame for these general observations. Goswami claims that the division of words on the page into syllables and the further division of syllables into initial consonant (onset) and final vowel (rime) units is useful when teaching children to read because:

> '*Onsets and rimes are an important part of a child's phonological (sound) awareness. Children's phonological awareness has been shown by research to be important for their reading progress so we need to develop their oral awareness of sound patterns in language*'.

Putting it another way, what Goswami recommends is that new readers learn words in rhyming groups, recognising the interaction of initial consonant clusters and succeeding vowels within syllables; the way that initial consonants influence the sound of the vowels which succeed them in speech production; capitalising upon the aural connections between similarly spelled morphemes as they are read aloud from the page. Rhyme is of course one of the core elements of poetry and the Poetry Society is on the brink of launching is own investigation into the benefit of phonological connection. *Playing with Poetry,* a creative reading and writing workshop for 4-7 year olds and their adult carers, designed by poet and counsellor Cheryl Moskovitz, promotes good practice in the earlier stages of reading. There are various other theoretical premises behind the use of a verbal artist in this context. There is value introducing different human speakers as opposed to synthesised voices to new young readers as they come to terms with the lack of acoustic invariance – the phonological relativism – inherent in human speech production and learn to connect symbols on a page with the very different sounds that different people use to represent them.

However, given the redesign of teaching schemes such as the Oxford Reading Tree to accommodate the importance of rhyme and analogy in reading acquisition, is there ary reason why a school or schools' consortium should use a poet in school rather than a fiction writer or a dramatist to facilitate children's learning? As the W.H. Smith Poets in Schools scheme run by the Poetry Society enters its twenty-fifth year, the reasons seem clear to those of us involved in the administration of this creative writing and reading programme. Of course, all the verbal arts have their merits but the writing of poetry is an art of great decision, precision and – generally – concision. There is usually little time or room to establish the context of a poem. This single utterance must suffice to communicate all the myriad meanings that its author wishes to convey. Consequently, its creation may require a more disciplined approach than that of a 'more roomy' play or piece of fiction. Poets who are thoughtful about their own linguistic processes are therefore well-prepared to aid teachers in facilitating the language development of others. Besides, as we said earlier, poetry can prove a concise medium; a vehicle to convey many messages about literacy, education and life.

Firstly, and most obviously, **Poetry is language with a purpose**. The rules, such as they are, which govern its writing demand an understanding of form and audience and some notion of how that meaning may be conveyed to the reader/listener. An ability to manipulate language for effect is predicated not just upon the understanding of syntax and semantics but requires an awareness of the importance of sound shared by anyone learning to read: who has ever tried to sound a word out in their first or another language. With regard to content, **Poetry is powerful**. Its reading or writing can be emotionally cathartic in times of stress. Anthologies such as *Stopping for Death* are potentially useful in the sort of bereavement counselling for the young recently advocated by the *TEX* whilst the Arts Council of England's poetry survey revealed that a majority of the people surveyed had written at least one poem in response to extreme emotion at some time in their adult lives.

More importantly, **Poetry is democratic, it can work with people of all ages and abilities**. In Birmingham, *Babies into Books* makes use of poetry books with very young children to promote family literacy. The Oxford University Press project headed by Dr Goswami has been covered at length elsewhere in the article whilst there is much anecdotal evidence about the use of shorter poems with dyslexic pupils, and disaffected boys. **Poetry can (also) be sociable or secret**. It works when spoken out loud collectively and when read from the page alone or in small groups. Ideally, successful speech acquisition facilitates successful reading acquisition but as the *Pen Down* project in Somerset demonstrates it is probably the prolonged professional contact implicit in supervising performance preparation or small group work which is most important.

Finally, and perhaps most importantly for the youngest learners, **Poetry is pleasurable** – always a form of linguistic play, whatever one's stage of development. It makes enjoyable use of the musicality inherent in language as we learn how to make words serve our own purposes. Perhaps at this point it's worth remembering that if children could learn to formalise and articulate their frustrations with life, indeed if we all learned to say what we mean through a socially acceptable medium like poetry, then they would be a chance to resolve conflict before it escalated and fewer of us would resort to physical force to express our frustrations. Perhaps we would reduce the chance of another Dunblane occurring.

Wishful thinking perhaps, but at time when there is increasing emphasis on the provision of educational opportunities for the under fives (yet a number of education authorities confess that the majority of infant pupils are educated in classes of more than thirty-five) rather than just waiting until we can provide the hardware which, a recent Labour Party survey tells us, only approximately 50% of primary school teachers are skilled to operate and for which few software packages yet exist, wouldn't it be simpler and cheaper to develop young people's basic literacy now by expanding schemes such as Poets in Schools? Certainly if such workshops were to become statutory provision, and if every child had the right to participate in at least one such workshop during their formal education, we might help to reintegrate poetry teaching into the English curriculum, a need acknowledged in the Education Reform Act of 1988. then perhaps we could finally begin to build on the wisdom of mothers' language work with children: rhymes and lullabies sung since time immemorial. Then we might enable teachers to familiarise themselves with an artform about which they report they are anxious – because they don't believe that they were sufficiently well-taught at school.

The introduction of statutory provision seems unlikely in the current political climate – and may always remain a pipe dream unless schools' budgets are drastically increased – but meanwhile, schools could think about banding together to form consortia – and applying to the lottery to fund poets in schools for themselves. Who knows, in three years' time we may realise that this has become (and should remain) one of our cheapest, most cost-effective tools, in the battle for universal literacy before we enter the next millennium.

30
Reading and Language Information Centre, University of Reading

Prue Goodwin, Viv Edwards

For almost 30 years, the Reading and Language Information Centre has been concerned with issues fundamental to the 'building of a literate nation'. The Centre came into being through the efforts of Betty Root who, in the very early days, took materials for the teaching of reading to schools so that teachers could make choices without pressure from publishers. As time went on, book selections which once fitted into the boot of a car developed into a permanent display which now stands at almost 14,000 in-print children's books, teacher's books, examples of educational software and audiovisual resources.

Each year the Centre produces 6-8 new publications on issues of topical concern which are distributed through a subscription scheme to some 4,000 primary schools all over the UK and beyond. We are also involved in literacy research. In the region of 5000 visitors come to the Centre every year, both to view the resources and to attend the extensive programme of courses and conferences which we offer to teachers, parents, governors, publishers and others concerned with literacy development.

Address: Reading and Language Information Centre, The University of Reading, Bulmershe Court, Earley, Reading RG6 1HY

Tel: 0113 931 8820 Fax: 0118 931 6801

Professional Development and the Teaching of Reading: An Agenda for the Next Five Years

Defining the problem

Our particular perspective on the agenda for literacy over the next five years is very much informed by our experience of INSET at the Centre. As the dust settles from the turbulent changes associated with the National Curriculum, we have a good opportunity to take stock. While impatient at the sometimes conflicting directives and the many impossible demands, most people now accept that the view of literacy which has emerged from the ensuing debate is much broader, richer and more challenging than was previously the case.

Children are now required to interact with text in a range of ways which are sometimes subsumed under the umbrella of 'higher order reading skills'. They are, for instance, required to retrieve information and to respond critically to the text. Expectations of children's writing are also very different. They need to write for different audiences and to produce writing in different fiction and non-fiction genres. They are also expected to look on writing as a craft or process which integrates the skills of transcription and composition. The arrival of IT in the classroom also raises many issues of importance for both reading and writing.

Teachers, for their part, have needed to develop strategies for helping children acquire a much wider range of literacy skills; they have also needed to acquire a sound understanding of the principles and practice of monitoring and assessment and how these apply to literacy development, as well as to other areas of the curriculum.

Colleagues involved with initial teacher education are already responding to new demands. However, we cannot overlook the needs of serving teachers. We have a workforce, many of whom have been teaching for a considerable time and yet have received very little training in the teaching of reading. Key stage 2 teachers face particular challenges. The recognition that literacy cannot be separated from other aspects of learning – and that all teachers in the primary years must necessarily be specialists in literacy development – is a relatively recent development.

In the past, when the teaching of reading was seen largely as the concern of key stage 1, the main focus for teachers working at key stage 2 will have been on encouraging children to read, and on the promotion of books. Such activities are important. However, we now understand that most children will not develop the levels of literacy required by society simply by being exposed to books: they also need ongoing learning experiences which help develop specific skills.

This raises questions about the kind of preparation that teachers need. Our experience tells us that there are three main ingredients: theoretical knowledge, practical application and confidence building.

Teachers need a firm theoretical basis from which to develop their practice. All too often, practical classroom strategies have been emphasised to the detriment of underlying theory. For instance, teachers with only a limited understanding of the rationale for approaches such as DARTs, or silent reading sessions, have sometimes put them into practice in inappropriate ways. When faced with disappointing results, they often resort to more traditional methods rather than trying to understand what has gone wrong.

Teachers need to understand the theoretical underpinnings of their practice; they also need the confidence to apply this knowledge to their own situation and, in particular, to individual children in their class. They need opportunities to explore how literacy develops, to challenge and question at their own level. Action research, in which teachers are invited to undertake a small-scale school-based project, forms an essential element of our longer courses. Having identified a theoretical issue pertinent to their own situation, they are asked to implement the necessary changes in classroom or school practice, and to observe and analyse what happens. This approach helps teachers to apply their new-found knowledge in eminently practical ways. By encouraging reflection, they develop a sounder understanding of the issues and a greater confidence in applying their new knowledge.

Confidence building is, of course, a major aim of any learning situation. However, it is particularly important in the context of a group of demoralised professionals who have been the target for unfair criticism from politicians and the popular press. Those responsible for in-service need to recognise the vulnerability of teachers as a group, and to build on their previous experience.

Setting the agenda

Experience of various GEST initiatives – jointly funded by central government and LEAs, and usually delivered in partnership with higher education institutions – offers useful insights into possible ways forward and, in particular, the need for a long-term and sustained strategy for the professional development of teachers.

The GEST programme for English, for instance, has created many opportunities for closing gaps in teachers' knowledge. Because these courses usually extend over several days, they give trainers the chance to explore a range of issues in far greater depth than would be the case on half or one day courses; they also offer participants space to reflect on their own situation and to exchange views and experiences with colleagues in other schools.

The main problem with GEST programmes, however, is that they offer very limited opportunities for long-term planning. The level of funding available for English has decreased over the last three years and seems likely to continue to do so. GEST, with all its uncertainties, can only be seen as a 'sticking plaster' solution for a very serious problem. Similar observations apply to the GEST programme on 'Meeting the Needs of Bilingual Pupils' in which Centre staff have been closely involved. However, all is not lost. Both GEST initiatives have made it possible to identify what needs most urgent attention and to develop appropriate content and strategies for courses. In the process a number of factors have emerged as vital for the effective professional development of teachers:

- realistic time-scales for courses: there is an urgent need to move away from 'quick fix' day or half day courses

- engagement: the chance for teachers to make new knowledge their own in a non-threatening environment

- action and reflection: the chance to apply the new knowledge to their own teaching situation

- follow-up: learning depends on reinforcement, whether we are teachers or children; one exposure is often not enough.

Any agenda for the next five years needs to engage with the above and recognise the cost implications.

31

The Reading Reform Foundation

Dr. Bonnie Macmillan

Secretary of the UK Chapter

The RRF is a non-profit making organisation whose sole aim is to help end today's needless illiteracy through the dissemination of the latest information about research-verified reading teaching. Intensive, systematic phonics teaching is promoted through a quarterly newsletter and occasional conferences. Annual membership, including subscription to the newsletter, is £10-00.

Contact: The Reading Reform Foundation, 2 Keats Avenue, Wiston, Prescott, Merseyside, L35 2XR.

Crisis Treatment: Reliable Evidence Must Direct the Teaching of Reading

The agenda for literacy

'Literacy' is defined by the Oxford English dictionary as the ability to read and write. However, since the ability to read underlies all writing-related skills, this discussion will focus on the teaching of reading. Whether a child learns to read will not only have a profound effect on his or her future individually but also on the future of the country as a whole. What, then, should be the agenda over the next five years for this important aspect of literacy? What is the present state of affairs with regard to the reading achievement of young children in this country? Is there room for improvement? And, if so, what steps should be taken to ensure that all young children learn to read, and read well?

The present standards of reading achievement among young children

Are teachers succeeding in teaching *all* children to read in the primary schools of this country? The age of 7 is the earliest stage for which we now have some indication of the reading achievement of young children. Reading test results both from subjective curriculum tests nationally and from objective standardised testing in many schools reveal an alarming rate of failure. After spending two years in school, national tests show that as many as 25 % to 30% of children are unable to read more than one word, while standardised testing conducted in some schools shows that up to 79% of children are failing to read after this period.[1] These rates of reading failure represent a serious crisis in our primary schools.

Indeed, failing to read by the age of 7 has far-reaching consequences. Studies show, rather than social or cultural factors, reading ability at age 7 is by far the most important factor influencing results at GCSE level.[2] Supporting this finding, a substantial amount of research evidence shows that a child's development in many other areas is significantly and progressively hindered by poor reading skills.[3]

The cause of reading failure

Why are so many children failing to read? Before one can determine how reading standards might be improved, some attempt to isolate the cause of the problem needs to be made.

Over the last ten or more years the concept of 'reading' has been redefined. Reading is no longer seen as the dual process of deciphering print accurately *and* making sense of it. Instead, the process of reading now involves the latter element only. Accurate decoding (making connections between print and sound) is no longer seen as important; making connections between print and meaning has become the exclusive aim.[4]

This new definition of reading has led to the adoption of a number of teaching practices which for many children simply do not work, and which contradict research evidence as to what methods do work, those which *are* able to produce a 100% success rate. Instead of an early focus on helping children to grasp the alphabetic principle, now overwhelmingly beyond dispute as *the* key requirement in teaching a child to read[5], there is instead, right from the beginning of school, the widespread use of the seemingly benign 'mixture of methods' to teach beginning reading.

However, reports and surveys which have examined the nature of current teaching practice reveal that this 'mixture' of methods is a myth: the mixture consists largely of various whole-word, memorisation and guessing methods.[6] Instead of direct, intensive, and comprehensive teaching of phonological skills and letter-phoneme knowledge, this information, if included, is taught sparingly, and incidentally. Instead of matching early reading materials closely with alphabetic knowledge taught, there is, in contrast, the use of either non-graded reading scheme books or 'real books' where children are encouraged to guess at, memorise words, or learn whole stories off by heart.

Thus, instead of possessing an effective, generative strategy for tackling new words, many children do not understand that print represents speech sounds, and that it can be translated into these speech sounds which one, then, can assimilate to form words. Instead of being given reading materials that match their alphabetic skills and that will enhance reading confidence, many children may quickly develop the idea that they are failures, and may suffer from the constant insecurity that comes from the much advocated practice of guessing at words through the use of context and picture cues. These unfruitful practices are not supported by research evidence.[7] Indeed, whole word memorisation and guessing strategies have been shown to produce deleterious effects on the level and rate of reading achievement.[8] Worse, other studies have demonstrated a direct correlation between the poor reading skills which result from such methods and aggressive or delinquent behaviour.[9]

What steps should be taken to improve reading standards?

If reading standards among young children are to improve, those in positions of responsibility should be certain that change to be implemented does not merely reflect what has become fashionable at the expense of what has been scientifically verified. The following changes are suggested:

- **Overhaul teacher training.** Ofsted and the TTA must introduce and monitor changes in the course content of teacher training institutions so that they reflect the findings from research demonstrating the efficacy of phonics-first methods. The current situation is such that[10]: not one book on a list of the top 30 most popular teacher training texts outlines how to teach a child to read in a manner supported by research, and 60% of trainees report that they are taught little or nothing about phonics. Furthermore, as a result of their training, all trainees believe that a mixture of methods should be used to teach reading right from the beginning and that encouraging children to enjoy books should take precedence over teaching children the skills needed to read them, both views which belie those held by their teacher trainers.

- **Re-educate practising teachers.** In-service training should be offered to practising teachers who may have been exposed not only to inadequate teacher training but to inadequate methods of reading instruction in their primary school years. These teachers should have the opportunity to take short intensive courses in grammar, spelling, punctuation, and in how to develop phonological and letter-phoneme skills in an early reading programme, one shown by comparative research to produce the highest levels of reading achievement.

• **Increase validity and reliability of testing and evaluation**. At the moment, national reading tests may simply be assessing the extent of a child's repertoire of whole-word strategies. Also, the failure to account for age differences and the subjective nature of evaluation means that reliable comparisons from year to year, or from school to school cannot be made.. The national, annual administration of a conventional (more valid), standardised, age 7+ reading test would allow such comparison and increase schools' commitment to improving standards. Such a test would save money: it would be cheaper than the current form of testing, and could replace Ofsted inspections as a reliable and objective indicator of a school's performance.

• **Reduce funding to fashion, increase funding to science**. The teaching procedures used or advocated by all government officials, colleges, schools, or charity groups which are now in receipt of government funding are in need of critical examination. Those who are well-informed and allow their actions to be driven only by empirical research knowledge should be rewarded; those who produce or encourage an ever-increasing number of failing readers through their lack of knowledge should no longer be rewarded with continued funding.

References

1. DES (1991), DFE (1992, 1994, 1995), DFEE (1996) Results of the National Curriculum assessments for 7 year-olds. London: HMSO.

   OFSTED (Office for Standards in Education). (1996) *The teaching of reading in 45 inner London primary schools. A report by Her Majesty 's Inspectorate in collaboration with the LEAs of Islington, Southwark and Tower Hamlets.*

2. Sammons, P., Nuttall, D., Cuttance, P., and Thomas, S. (1993). *Continuity of school effects. A longitudinal analysis of primary and secondary school effects on GCSE performance.* Institute of Education, University of London, Department of Curriculum Studies.

3. For example, Stanovich, K. (1986) Matthew effects in reading: Some consequences of individual differences in the acquisition of literacy. *Reading Research Quarterly,* 21, 360407.

4. For example:

   Brooks, G., Pugh, A.K., and Schagen, I. (1996) *Reading performance at nine.* Slough: NFER.

Webster, A., Beveridge, M., and Reed, M. (1996) Conceptions of literacy in primary and secondary school teachers. *Journal of Research in Reading*, 19(1). 36-45.

5. For review:

Rieben, L. and Perfetti, C.(1991) *Learning to read: Basic research and its implications*. NJ: Erlbaum.

Gough, P. B., Ehri, L., and Treiman, R. (1992) (Eds.), *Reading acquisition*. NJ:Erlbaum.

6. Cato, V., Fernandes, C., Gorman, T. Kispal, A., and White, J. (1992) *The teaching of initial literacy: How do teachers do it?* Slough: NFER.

Various HMI and Ofsted reports: for review, see Macmillan, B. (1997) *Why Schoolchildren Can't Read*. London: The Institute of Economic Affairs.

7. For example, Nicholson, T. (1991) Do children read words better in context or in lists? A classic study revisited. *Journal of Educational Psychology*, 83(4), 444-450.

8. For review:

Adams, M. J. (1990) *Beginning to read: Thinking and learning about print*. Cambridge, MA:MIT Press.

Chall, J. S. (1989) *Learning to read: The great debate 20 years later – A response to 'debunking the great phonics myth'*. Phi Delta Kappa, March, 521-537.

9. For example:

Barber, M. (1996) *Young people and their attitudes to school: An interim report of a research project in the centre for successful schools*. Keele: Keele University.

Brunner, M. S. (1993) *Retarding America*. Portland, Oregon: Halcyon House.

10. Brooks, G., Gorman, T., Kendall, L. and Tate, A. (1992) *What teachers in training are taught about reading: The working papers*. National Foundation for Educational Research.

32

Research and Practice in Adult Literacy (RaPAL)

Mary Hamilton, *Chair*, Julia Clarke, Margaret Herrington,
Gaye Houghton and David Barton

The Research and Practice in Adult Literacy group is an independent network of learners, teachers, managers and researchers in adult basic education and literacy across the post-16 sector. Established in 1985, it is supported by membership subscription only.

RaPAL campaigns for the rights of all adults to have access to the full range of literacies in their lives.

RaPAL encourages collaborative and reflective research that is closely linked with practice. We work in partnership with others committed to developing a learning democracy.

RaPAL produces a newsletter three times a year and other occasional publications. We organise an annual conference. We contribute to national debates about literacy, actively challenging public myths, developing and publicising alternative views.

Address: Research and Practice in Adult Literacy (RaPAL) Gaye Houghton, The Secretary, 124 Town Lane, Whittle-le-Woods, Chorley, Lancs. PR6 8AG

Building a Learning Democracy

What do we mean by 'building a literate nation'?

RaPAL approaches the idea of 'building a literate nation' with a broad and open conception of the literacies that exist within the many diverse communities of the UK. Effective literacy actions (programmes and policies) should enable people to participate in the literacies in their homes and workplaces, in public life, leisure and educational settings.

Over the last ten years, adult basic education (ABE) has become a permanent part of formal educational provision in the UK, subject to outcome-related funding, quality criteria, standardised accreditation and a vocational slant to courses. These developments have taken place in a very different climate from that which framed the original 'right to read' campaign of the the 1970's.

An emphasis on competition, and on individual, market-led solutions to social problems has led to the erosion of democratic mechanisms, fragmentation of community initiatives, fewer collective and public resources. A significant minority of the population faces increasing poverty and social exclusion. RaPAL believes that these changes weaken the culture of literacy and must be overcome by any literacy policy.

Improved access to literacy is blocked by the narrow and simplistic definitions of literacy which define it. They cause confusion about what literacy can really achieve in terms of social and economic change and are used to exclude many literacies from public recognition. RaPAL believes that there is an urgent need for a change of discourse in policy and media circles. One of our priorities is to debate the many uses and meanings of literacy so as to develop alternatives to guide our actions.

RaPAL looks beyond individual skills to the social practices involved in a literate culture and supports theories of language and literacy learning which take account of social context and build on diversity. What people *can* do interests us more than what they cannot do. Learning takes place not only in classrooms but in other social settings. Therefore we look beyond education and teaching methods to other official settings and to the vernacular practices and informal learning in which literacies play a key role. We look beyond 'literature' to a wider view of culture; beyond print literacy to other media and forms of representation.

We aim to develop a clear understanding of how literacy is part of the social and economic reality of people's lives, placing it in its broader context of institutional purposes and power relationships. From this perspective, the main issue is not one of literacy standards but of understanding and dealing with economic, technological and social change and the social exclusion resulting from these changes.

Adult Basic Education students have much to offer in judging school-based literacy practices: they know what didn't work for them and can see the impact of exclusionary educational practice in their own lives. Their participation in the decision-making processes of policy, practice and research is essential.

What are realistic priorities for the next 5 years?

In general, we need a coherent policy for literacy that assumes the right of access to the full range of literacies, for adults and our children. This involves a serious commitment from all partners to financing and implementing it. RaPAL's approach carries clear implications for such a policy at a number of levels, within and between institutions.

Specifically we suggest a strategic agenda that includes:

• A critical examination of the messages about literacy circulating in the media (print, TV and film) with a view to changing negative and simplistic images about literacy and about those with specific learning difficulties

• A comparative review of literacy learning opportunities for adults across the UK regions and internationally, to encourage creative thinking about supporting adults who have many linked goals including citizenship, social participation in workplace, and public life. International experience can help us develop our understanding of the global influences on local policy decisions and widen our ideas of the range of possible strategies

- Designing institutional frameworks which support the development of a culture of literacy and access to it for all. Literacy is not just an educational issue: many institutions should be involved in partnerships for cultural action, crossing traditional boundaries, such as those between libraries, arts and community publishing projects and those linked with practical social action – such as housing and other social services, advice centres, legal and medical organisations. Businesses and unions could also make a greater contribution

- Support for a range of adult learning opportunities which will provide stepping stones from informal to formal learning for those who need them. For this we need to develop a productive and complementary relationship between statutory and voluntary organisations. Strong democratic consultation and decision-making mechanisms are essential to the development of learning programmes which can respond to the diversity of knowledge and uses of literacy among all adults and their communities, including other media and other languages and cultures, developing writing as well as reading

- Promotion of research and development skills and strategies, with resources devolved to local communities for this purpose. Linking research, teaching and learning promotes a learning democracy, challenges myths and opens debate about the meanings and goals of literacy programmes

- Dealing with staff development as a policy issue by means of programmes linked to higher education which can produce reflective professionals with a real sense of community who can contribute to policy formation. Staff development should include opportunities for both paid and volunteer staff and should be linked with strong networks, improved conditions of work and career progression. It should facilitate recruitment of staff from a broad range of backgrounds. Insights from ABE should be included in all teacher training programmes

- Resisting the imposition of mono-cultural, monolingual approaches to literacy education by putting in place programmes that recognise and build on the resources that are available in multi-lingual communities. Being able to communicate in more than one language is a desirable goal for all UK citizens

- A critique of sterile notions of competency-based education and training. Insistence on alternative forms of assessment and measures of quality including input and process as well as output. Explore assessment practices which use different modes of communication (oral and visual as well as written) and build on the experience of Open Colleges around the country that have found flexible ways of accrediting courses, tailored to local needs.

Conclusion

In the past, adult education and training has been kept on the margins of social policy. This means that those who get least from initial education have least access to learning opportunities later in life. While RaPAL welcomes new links between adult and child literacy through, for example, family literacy programmes, we think it is essential to keep a focus on adults. We live most of our lives as adults, meeting many new demands on our literacies at different times. In the many depleted communities of turn-of-the-millennium Britain, poverty and stress limit peoples aspirations as they struggle with the day-to-day tasks of survival. By supporting lifelong learning, adult-literacy programmes can enlarge people's own vision of their lives and communities and strengthen the resources available to them to achieve their goals.

Mary Hamilton, Julia Clarke, Margaret Herrington, Gaye Houghton and David Barton on behalf of the Research and Practice in Adult Literacy working group.

33

School Library Association

Graham Small

National Committee

The School Library Association will celebrate its Diamond Jubilee in 1997. For the past sixty years it has been supporting and encouraging all those committed to the promotion and development of libraries in schools. It campaigns to ensure appropriate provision for school libraries and school library services and provides a significant voice to focus attention at regional and national level.

It provides training workshops and seminars for school library staff.

In liaison with the Paul Hamlyn Foundation it administers school library award schemes. It has also established, in liaison with the Library Association, the School Libraries Forum which brings together for regular discussion representatives from a wide range of educational and publishing groups.

It publishes a quarterly journal 'The School Librarian' which has a supplement reviewing CD-ROMS and other information technology media.

Address: School Library Association, Liden Library, Barrington Close, Liden, Swindon, Wiltshire SN3 6HF. Telephone: 01793 617838.

Book Rogers in the 21st Century: School Libraries, Past, Present and Future – A Personal View

In the Beginning

If we cast our minds back to our own schooldays I am sure we all have a shared memory of the school library being a place with books in it at the end of a corridor. It was usually unstaffed, and, when not being used for teaching, was where teachers sent difficult pupils. Sometimes English teachers would be asked if they wouldn't mind 'looking after the library', because it would look good on a CV, and, after all, libraries are about reading. Stock usually came from donations, jumble sales, or grants from the PTA.

Matters improved slightly during the 60s and 70s, with a few enlightened LEAs taking the lead in establishing School Library Services and placing qualified librarians in schools

Then, in the 80s, the tide turned in our favour. The LISC report, School Libraries: The Foundation of the Curriculum, was published in 1984[1]. This placed school libraries firmly at the centre of educational provision. This was followed by the introduction of GCSEs with their emphasis on resource-based learning. Then, in 1988, came the Education Reform Act and the National Curriculum, with its insistence that all pupils need to know how to find and use information.

Between a rock and a hard place

So where are we now?

On the plus side, we have the revised National Curriculum, with an increased emphasis on finding and using information, we have GNVQs at 14, and a small but steady increase in the number of qualified librarians being employed in schools[2]. We also have Coopers and Lybrand recommending that School Library Services be funded centrally[3].

On the negative side, the recommendations of the LISC report have still not been implemented, and the Department of National Heritage reports that library provision for children and young people is in a very poor state[4].

To Boldly Go...........

So how do I see school libraries developing into the 21st century?

Ask this question around the profession and there seem to be two basic responses, one high tech. optimistic, the other low tech. pessimistic. The first sees us leaping onto the information technology rollercoaster for a whizz-bang ride on the Internet, with CD-Roms and on-line database links, all handled by pupils and teachers working from individual workstations, remote from a central library or even off site altogether. The second sees us left behind in the race to be technocrats and sidelined by computer people, leaving us, if employed at all, blowing the dust off unused and fading parchments in some forgotten corner of the high tech., industry-oriented school of the future. I subscribe to neither of these views

I see our future growing from the strength of our role in education. Traditionally, we play a central role in supporting and promoting literacy. Professionally, our business is information. The two are indivisible. We are about showing people how to find – and use – information effectively. For this, literacy is a fundamental requirement

We are there to guide pupils, and, let's be honest, teachers, through the increasingly complicated web that is information, in all its forms. As pupils are asked to take on greater responsibility for their own research, so our expertise will increasingly be at a premium. We already have the National Curriculum, GCSEs, GNVQs, and soon we shall have the revised GCSE A-Levels. The general trend is away from rote learning towards supported self-study, and it is here that we come into our own

As regards information technology, these are the tools of our trade. I welcome them. But we should never be so dazzled by the bells and whistles of these wonderful toys into thinking that they can replace what we already have. Last year, CD-Rom was vaunted as the 'library of the future'. This year, the Internet is flavour of the month. Next year, I am sure, something else will come along. They all have their role to play, but none of them – of themselves – can provide what all of them can provide when used appropriately. They are additional tools in our continually growing toolbox

The school library in the 21st century will provide a mixture of traditional and electronic information sources in a variety of media. It is likely to be managed by a qualified librarian, with clerical support. It will be busy, with groups booked in during class times and individuals using it throughout the day. It will be used as a centre for independent study and research. The school librarian will offer advice on the availability and use of information sources, and will guide pupils in their private reading. Its role in the education process will be recognised and supported by both the teaching staff and the pupils

If this vision sounds familiar it is because it is already here. What I have described is present day best practice – the kind of library advocated by HMI[5]. The difference between now and then will be the number of libraries matching this description. As time goes by, academic and financial pressures will push schools towards this because it offers both high academic standards and cost effectiveness. As these pressures grow, as they surely will, more schools will be writing this into their development plans and, as the century progresses, this will become the rule rather than the exception.

The End of the Beginning

We have come a long way from that place at the end of the corridor, but we still have some way to go before we reach the status and position that reflects the importance of our role. That will not come until school libraries are made a mandatory service. Until then, the educational tide is running in our favour, although the resources may not always be available to support it. The increase in the number of qualified librarians in schools shows that, where the money can be made available, the financial will is there. What is lacking is the political will to back it up.

Until it is, we must weather the storm and show how money spent on us is money well spent – financially as well as educationally. We have achieved a lot in the past ten years. The next century is three years away. Just think what can be achieved by then!

References

1. Office of Arts and Libraries (1984) *School Libraries: the Foundation of the Curriculum*, HMSO.

2. Creaser, Claire (1994,1995) *A Survey of Library Services to Schools and Children in the UK*, LISU.

3. Cooper and Lybrand/Department of National Heritage (1995) *School Library Services and Financial Delegation to Schools*. HMSO.

4. Department of National Heritage Investing in Children (1995) *The future of Library Services for Children and Young People* (Library Information Series No. 22). HMSO.

5. Department of Education and Science (1989) *Better Libraries: Good Practice in Schools – A Survey by HM Inspectorate*. HMSO.

This article is an abridgement of an article that first appeared in The School Librarian, August 1995.

34
Scottish Community Education Council (SCEC)

Charlie McConnell

Executive Director

The Scottish Community Education Council is the national agency for community education in Scotland, a term encompassing community-based education services in the fields of youth work, adult education and community work delivered primarily by local authorities and voluntary sector organisations.

The primary functions of the Council are to influence public policy and awareness, promote effective strategies and best practice, and provide information, publications and other services. It is also responsible for ensuring training standards at all levels in the field of community education.

The Council's vision is to contribute to a society where lifelong learning provision enables people to make informed choices and work together to improve the quality of life for all.

Address: Scottish Community Education Council, Rosebery House, 9 Haymarket Terrace, Edinburgh, EH12 5EZ

Tel:0131 313 2488, Fax: 0131 313 6800

The Agenda for Scotland

The recent development of basic skills in Scotland can be related directly to the successful BBC television campaign 'On the Move', launched in 1975. Subsequent Government funding supported an extensive advertising campaign, a network of telephone referral points, and encouraged local authorities to appoint organisers to recruit, train and deploy volunteer tutors.

At local level adult literacy provision became an established part of the local authority Community Education Services providing individual and group teaching and learning, now known as Adult Basic Education or Essential Learning Skills.

However, in recent years the lack of sufficient and sustained central Government investment, in comparison with England and Wales, together with a major restructuring of local government in April 1996 has led to the fragmentation of provision and loss of many of these specialist services. As a result, adult literacy has been pushed back down the agenda both nationally and locally. In England, for example, the national Basic Skills Agency receives £4.5 million per annum from central government, an investment not available in Scotland.

Yet at the same time, the Advisory Scottish Council for Education and Training Targets have set standards of achievement for the year 2000 recognising that these cannot be met without improving our country's literacy base. The Higher Still Development Programme, which aims to improve the quality of post-16 education for all students through the unification and rationalisation of the academic and vocational education systems, promotes the value and place of core skills (communication, numeracy, personal effectiveness and problem-solving, and information technology) across the curriculum.

The challenges facing people with literacy needs grow as the education and training levels required to meet the demands of the workplace and to exercise the rights and responsibilities of citizenship in an increasingly complex society rise.

What can be done? The Scottish Adult Basic Education/Essential Skills Group – a network of managers and practitioners from the 32 new Councils in Scotland, established in 1996 – is calling for a national programme to support basic skills needs in Scotland with, as a priority, a similar investment by government as exists in England and Wales.

Scotland urgently needs:

A National Resource

For basic skills in Scotland to achieve the high profile necessary to change public perceptions and to give real direction and development support to basic skills practitioners, an effective national resource must be created. Relating to both adult and child literacy and numeracy, the resource would require central Government support and would play a dynamic role in:

- supporting the right of every individual to receive free, local and accessible help with basic skills

- developing a quality assurance framework which would provide a minimum set of qualitative standards for use by basic skills providers and a structure for monitoring and evaluating provision

- marketing and publicising basic skills provision, promoting positive images of literacy learning by adults as an aspect of lifelong learning

- creating a bank of good practice and the development of Scottish-based materials and resources which would include materials relating to methods of widening access and strategies for targeting specific client groups

- investing in Family Literacy schemes which are proving to be successful at breaking the intergenerational cycle of underachievement in literacy and numeracy skills

- developing a nationally recognised qualification for basic skills tutors which could open up a career structure for tutors within community education and related fields

- undertaking a programme investigating literacy needs in Scotland.

An Investigation of Literacy Needs

Research into the literacy needs of the Scottish adult population has been identified as a priority. Without evidence of literacy needs or the types of problems adults have and how these arise and develop, it is difficult to sustain funding for services and to plan effective learning provision.

Literacy research, where it has been undertaken, has in the main concentrated on national surveys producing quantitative evidence of the scale of literacy needs. The Basic Skills Agency has recently carried out a number of important studies to test the functional literacy and numeracy skills held by the population in England and Wales and thereby make an assessment of need. Scotland has not been included in this research because the Basic Skills Agency's remit does not extend here. Adults in Scotland have formed part of the sample of 3,800 British adults surveyed in 1996 for an international quantitative study of literacy needs by the Organisation for Economic Co-operation and Development. Based on a bus timetable test, the results of this study, to be published by the Office for National Statistics during 1997, are likely to produce further statistical evidence on the proportion of adults who experience difficulties with reading, writing, spelling or numeracy.

Though providing valuable information, this type of research does not help us to understand the behaviours and attitudes around literacy, the needs of learners and the users of literacy services and the effects on the individual, workplace and society. Without hard evidence of the needs the problem cannot be tackled and the disenfranchisement and alienation of a growing number of adults in Scotland will continue, as will increasing skill shortages in areas necessary for a successful Scottish economy.

Building on the findings of previous quantitative studies researching literacy levels, it is proposed that a comparative, qualitative investigation should now be undertaken which would improve our understanding of the current literacy needs of the Scottish adult population. This investigation would explore the contexts for adult literacy through consultations with employers and with the users, potential users and non-users of literacy services. The research would look at the literacy experiences and aspirations of both men and women from a range of age groups and backgrounds, living in industrial, post-industrial and rural locations across Scotland.

The first step in the investigation would be to carry out an audit of relevant research conducted by the Basic Skills Agency and other literacy and literacy-related organisations.

The main focus of the research would be an exploration of the range of literacy needs demanded of people in the changing world of work and in a more complex society from the perspectives of employers, community leaders and, crucially from the learners, potential users and non-users of literacy services.

The investigation would look at the current literacy needs of the workplace and the community and would explore the literacy problems which adults perceive they have and at the ways in which difficulties arise and develop. The educational guidance needs of people experiencing literacy problems would be examined together with an exploration of the reasons why some people with literacy needs seek provision and others do not.

The research would aim to isolate both the factors which enable some people to adapt to the rising literacy requirements in the workplace and those which prevent people attaining the necessary literacy levels needed to cope with the new ways of working. The research would also explore the extent to which literacy is a factor affecting people's ability or desire to participate in society, measured in terms of exercising the right to vote, parenting, involvement in community events, local or national campaigns, voluntary work or another arena of civic life.

• The research findings would be discussed with employers, community leaders and education and training providers at regional seminars with a view to identifying effective learning strategies and provision, unmet literacy needs and areas for further development

• An authoritative and current resource of essential information on the literacy needs of the Scottish adult population would be available to employers, policymakers and education and training providers. Critical data of this nature would enable education services and employers to develop appropriate strategies and teaching and learning support to meet the literacy needs of the Scottish adult population.

Achieving the Agenda

The way forward for Scotland is to persuade policymakers and politicians at both local and national government levels of the need to invest in basic skills provision. The Scottish Community Education Council, the Government's national agency for adult education, and the agency which in the 1980's had responsibility for supporting Adult Basic Education has called for a national resource along the lines of the Basic Skills Agency and has urged the Scottish Office to undertake national research and development in this area, a call supported by the Scottish Adult Education Forum and senior managers in Scotland's local authority adult education services.

35

United Kingdom Reading Association (UKRA)

Dr Sue Beverton

Sue Beverton is president for 1996/7 of the United Kingdom Reading Association (UKRA). This is an association whose membership has been drawn predominantly from those with interests in the primary education sector, either as teachers or as teacher-educators. This is now broadening to include a wider diversity of membership. The views she presents here are her own, although she attempts to demonstrate how the UKRA has moved steadily towards supporting inter-professional collaboration over recent years. Her main point is that knowledge about literacy development has now reached such a degree of maturity that cross-fertilisation between different professional groupings of ideas, understanding and skills is now incumbent upon us all.

Address: United Kingdom Reading Association (UKRA) Contact Beryl Malins (Admin. Secretary), 'River View' Downing Road, Whitford, Nr. Holywell, Flintshire CH8 9EQ. Tel/Fax: 01745 561959.

Professional Collaboration – What Does the Future Hold?

UKRA was founded over thirty years ago, in the early sixties, when growth rates of knowledge about reading and of ideas about how the teaching of reading might be achieved were very high. In particular, universities and colleges of education were active in proposing and debating new methods of teaching reading. Indeed, a number of UKRA's earliest members, who include Joyce Morris, Donald Moyle and Derek Thackery, may be seen as taking up different positions in the debate. During the current decade, this debate has received renewed media and political attention, not always motivated by purely educational reasons. Throughout this period UKRA has preferred not to align itself with one view, rather, it has broadened its scope and moved its own centre of gravity, so to speak, to the area of literacy development across a wider range of learners. This mirrors a shift of focus which has occurred in the education world at large.

This shift has not been unproblematic. There are plenty of potentially contentious issues in aspects of literacy development other than the ones concerned with the teaching of reading, such as how and when to introduce cursive writing, different ways of teaching spelling and the impact of a National Curriculum, SATs and Teacher Assessment upon literacy learning. A consequence of this shift, for both UKRA in particular and for the literacy development field in general, has been the need to create lines of communication with the many other professional groups whose interests also lie within the same field. This may be a logical necessity – if you increase the scope of your professional interests, then you will be brought into contact with more groups of other professionals – but is fascinating to see how there has been a redefining of which professionals have legitimate claims to holding interests in literacy development, It is even more fascinating to witness the mix of different professional backgrounds actually happening.

I would like to demonstrate this through considering one type of inter-professional collaboration and development, Family Reading Groups

(FRGs), although I know many other types can and do exist. In 1993 UKRA produced a short guide (Beverton et al.) to help teachers who were interested in running 'Family Reading Groups'. These are informal groups of teachers and /or librarians or other professionals, parents and children which focus on enjoying books. The guide was the outcome of a three year project which received (then) DES funding to look into how such small groups functioned successfully. The aim of Family Reading Groups is to foster a love of reading. They run along the lines of after-school clubs, although many were found which were attached to libraries, nurseries and playgroups. Their focus is the enjoyment of books in a group setting with family members and teachers, librarians and often, community workers. FRGs are not extensions of school, they do not aim to teach reading, but teachers do find that the excitement and book-related interest they generate is beneficial for reading.

While not organised in any national sense, leaders of Family Reading Groups consistently reported to the project workers that collaboration with other professionals brought valued and unexpected gains. Clear cases of this regularly came in the form of a teacher and a children's librarian either leading FRG meetings together or working side by side in planning, managing and reviewing the FRG meetings. Teachers said that they had not realised the skills and expertise that children's librarians possessed, and that they felt professionally developed through working with another professional who was not a teacher. It was a broadening experience, helping to clarify to the teachers what their own implicit theories of literacy development were and serving to increase their under-standing of how librarianship skills relate closely to their own area of professionalism.

Librarians reported similar benefits. They felt enriched through the experience of using their professional knowledge of children's books, authors and publishers in an educational setting. The project workers noted their enthusiasm and how positively and constructively such collaborating teams functioned.

Another professional group which came to the project's attention as working successfully in FRGs in some parts of the country was that of community workers, although other designations for similar roles do exist. In areas such as Greater Manchester, these were professionals appointed by Local Authorities under funding arrangements specifically to support families for whom English is a second language. At times working alongside librarians and/or teachers, FRGs were found to be productive vehicles for raising community literacy participation. Again, the project workers were struck by the enthusiasm generated when different professionals worked together.

My point is that there is a lesson here for both inter- and intra- professional collaboration in the future. The evidence I am drawing upon was gathered in the late eighties and early nineties. Now, at the time of writing, it is barely three years to the end of the decade. Indeed, the beginning of a new millennium is well within the range of policy makers across all aspects of our educational and social systems. Strategic plans are the places where new ideas can begin to be incorporated as formal arrangements. The FRG study found that the single biggest problem was that such inter-professional working together was ground-breaking. No model existed for teachers (who were necessarily stepping out of their professional settings and habitual roles) to surrender their autonomy, pool their ideas with librarians or community support workers (who were not, it has to be said, stepping so far out of habitual settings and roles), or, indeed, parents, and arrive democratically at decisions and plans for running meetings. Even more indicative was the difficulty of purchasing resources through any official bilateral arrangement. On the basis of professional goodwill, teachers often gave of their time to be involved in FRGs, while other professionals had broader interpretations as to what constituted professional activity, and FRGs were to them integral to their normal routine.

This lack of easy, ready-made lines of communication in working together is regrettable and reflects the compartmentalisation of views, attitudes and practice which has so strongly characterised our education culture. As long as this situation remains, literacy development on a national scale in this country risks being restricted, perhaps stifled, by the separatism of professional groupings. I would like to advocate an inclusive approach to involvement in literacy development, a release from the harnessed thinking to which policy-makers and planners are so attached and a deliberate opening-up of a broad front of involved and committed professionals.

I am not so naive as to believe this could be achieved only through top-down directives. Nor do I believe that a bottom-up type of action can grow sufficiently to gain acceptance and become absorbed into our national structures. I would say simultaneous action is needed. What we need is encouragement and support for an admixture from G.Ps, educational psychologists, speech therapists and nursery nurses to the kinds of cross-professional collaboration which can already be found, if only patchily distributed. It might also require greater vertical liaison within professions. For example, teachers in nurseries, infant, junior and secondary schools and even in colleges of further education, might gain from a greater sharing of their skills and understanding. In both kinds of scenario parity of esteem is essential.

A cynic might well sniff disparagingly at these two pleas for our society's future literacy development. Yet major cultural and attitudinal changes in our society can happen, usually when the demands of expediency at policy level coincide with developments in good educational practice. The rapid rise in the last decade of parental involvement in early years education is an example. The history of parental involvement is not a smooth one, however, and can result in conflict with other interested parties rather than constructive collaboration. Some consequences of the Code of Practice for the identification and assessment of Special Educational Needs, and the Education Act of 1993, are a case in point.

Despite this example, and away from its resources-driven nature, promising ground-level work with parents is being undertaken across the country in home-school partnerships. Why not broaden such work into cross-professional groupings? The lead must now come from the politicians, planners and decision makers. A cross-professional framework for literacy development must be established in which consultation and collaboration must be the keynote.

36
Volunteer Reading Help (VRH)

Charles Martineau

Director

Volunteer Reading Help selects and trains volunteers from the community who go twice a week to their local primary school to give regular individual help and encouragement to children who are having difficulty with their reading. They talk, read, play games and help to build each child's confidence and interest in books.

The children who benefit most from VRH include:

* those with little confidence

* underachievers

* those for whom English is a second language

* those with little parental support

Teachers choose the children to be helped.

There are 27 branches with 1400 VRHs helping 4,200 children in nearly 700 schools.

By 2000 we plan to be giving individual help to 10,000 children in 1,750 schools.

The cost for each child is under £100.

Address: Volunteer Reading Help, High Holborn House, 52/54 High Holborn, LONDON, WC1V 6RL

Telephone/Fax: 0171 404 6204

Tackling the Problem of Underachievement in Reading

The purpose of this paper is to make a contribution towards the agenda of when, how, where and by whom the problem of underachievement in reading should be tackled. There will always be a small percentage of people who, for various reasons, have genuine difficulty in deciphering the written word however much they may want to read. These people need specialist help. This paper will concentrate on the very large percentage of people who, for one reason or another, are failing to reach their full potential of reading ability.

When should the problem of underachievement in reading be tackled?

It is never too late to learn to read. However, the earlier a child is introduced to books and encouraged to read, the better it is. Any child whose reading age at the age of eleven is two years behind their chronological age will find difficulties in benefiting from secondary education. Indeed much of the investment in secondary education on such a child could be wasted. Although it is important to give help to those over eleven who have a low reading age, it is a much better investment in time and effort to tackle the problem earlier. Research has shown that the age of six is the most effective time to improve the reading age of a child who is behind in reading and Reading Recovery targets this age group. To concentrate all support for underachievers at this one age would not be helpful for everybody as children can decide to want to read at different ages. However, as children who are behind in reading grow older, there are ever more pressures on them and it becomes increasingly hard to build their self-esteem and encourage motivation.

How should the problem of underachievement in primary schools be tackled?

Teaching underachieving children to read is highly skilled and requires time. There are many techniques and many resource bases with the aim of obtaining the attention of the child. Different techniques and different resources will appeal to different children and it is the question of building on the strengths of each child. But if the child does not want to read, he or she will not read. This paper does not propose to discuss the techniques of teaching reading, but how to change the attitude of the child to be taught.

The child must be encouraged to want to read. Reading must be made fun. It can be that the problem will be lack of motivation and lack of self-esteem. It can be that there is no such thing as a book in their home or the child has no parental support or encouragement to read.

Learning to read should be as natural to any child as learning to ride a bike. Some children find it easy to ride a bike and some quite hard, but those who do find it hard do not give up. They keep on trying as they can see what fun it is. They want to learn as their friends ride bikes and more than likely they are encouraged by their parents. Learning to read should be just the same. The process of learning is very much longer and may not be as exciting, but the rewards should be many times greater. There will still be sense of achievement and enjoyment when a new book is finished. All children should want to read, and those that find it difficult should have all the help and encouragement they need.

For many children who have difficulties in learning to read there needs to be a change in their attitude, a change in attitude that brings about motivation that will make it so very much easier to teach them to read. This can be achieved by building up the self-esteem of these children through mentoring and showing that reading can be fun, possible and useful.

Where should the problem of underachievement be tackled?

The teaching of reading for most children takes place in the classroom. These children are taught by trained and skilled teachers. Some children are taught to read by their parents at home. Most children have some kind of help or support with their reading from someone who is better at reading than they are. This may take place in the classroom but is just as likely to take place elsewhere. It is important that underachievers do not link reading with a classroom alone. Indeed there are advantages that the help and support for a poor reader takes place somewhere other than in the classroom which can so easily be identified by these children with failure, with boredom, perhaps with fear or even with anger. To them it is not a very friendly environment and reading could never become a pleasure in such a place.

Reading is not confined to school and it should be demonstrated to under-achievers that help is everywhere for them. Reading is not ploughing your way through course readers. Reading enables you to enjoy the magic of wonderful books, read out some jokes from a joke book, read the instructions for a game and read what is on television that night.

Children having difficulty with their reading should be taught to read in the classroom. The help and support that these children need to build up their self-confidence can happen elsewhere. Any mentoring a child may have should take place outside the classroom.

Who should be involved in tackling the problem?

Children having difficulty learning to read should be taught by trained teachers. The help and support that these children need can come from anyone who can read better than they can. This can range from parents and other adults to children of their own age who are better at reading. This support can range from hearing the children read to mentoring a child on a regular basis. In all cases the child is being encouraged to read, but just as there are techniques in teaching a child to read, so there are techniques in building up a child's self-esteem and motivation.

Class teachers have a challenging time teaching classes of children of differing abilities. Smaller classes, improved facilities and better resources could help them in their task. But teachers are not the only people who can help to improve the level of literacy. Parents and the local community can play a major part and their contribution will be more valuable if they receive training for their role.

Training and support should be given to all these volunteers, whether they are hearing children reading or mentoring underachievers. There is a vast untapped resource within every community which with proper training and support can make a major contribution in improving the level of literacy of primary school children.

Summary

Children of primary school age who are underachieving should have regular additional help and support from adults other than their teachers. These adults should be trained to build the self-confidence of these children and show them that reading can be fun.